THE
7 PILLARS
OF GOD'S
WISDOM

THE 7 PILLARS OF GOD'S WISDOM

HERBERT LOCKYER

WHITAKER HOUSE

THE 7 PILLARS OF GOD'S WISDOM

ISBN: 978-1-60374-837-7
eBook ISBN: 978-1-60374-838-4
Printed in the United States of America
© 2013 by Ardis A. Lockyer

Whitaker House
1030 Hunt Valley Circle
New Kensington, PA 15068
www.whitakerhouse.com

Library of Congress Cataloging-in-Publication Data (pending)

1 2 3 4 5 6 7 8 9 10   ⨆⨆   19 18 17 16 15 14 13

CONTENTS

Introduction: The Significance of the Seven Pillars................................7

1. The Pillar of Mystery..13

2. The Pillar of Incarnation..37

3. The Pillar of Vindication..73

4. The Pillar of Revelation..79

5. The Pillar of Proclamation 117

6. The Pillar of Belief...125

7. The Pillar of Glorification..131

Conclusion: The Fundamental Spiritual Value of
   the Mystery We Confess..151

About the Author...159

INTRODUCTION

THE SIGNIFICANCE OF THE SEVEN PILLARS

In the book of Proverbs, Solomon declares, "*Wisdom has built her house*" and "*set up her seven pillars*" (Proverbs 9:1). Who is this figure whom he personifies as *Wisdom*, and what are these pillars that uphold the house of the wise person?

Solomon's poetic imagery is incomparable. His striking figures of speech describing persons and precepts, virtues and vices, are unique and unsurpassable. The passage of Proverbs 8:1–9:6 is a sterling example. In it, Solomon exalts the quality of wisdom and personifies it as a worker who was at God's side when He created the world, and who was daily His delight. The delights of wisdom herself, he adds, are "*with the sons of men*" (Proverbs 8:31 KJV): If they find her, they find life. "*Counsel is mine, and sound wisdom*" (verse 14 KJV), she says, and then Solomon affirms that she has built a house resting upon seven hewn-out pillars.

Even though Solomon cloaks this figure in such rich imagery, the spiritual mind has no difficulty in identifying personified wisdom as Christ, "*whom God made our wisdom, our righteousness and sanctification and redemption*" (1 Corinthians 1:30).

First, it should not surprise us to find Christ *depicted as a person* even in Old Testament times. The Scriptures record how the Lord God occasionally appeared both in angelic and human form during those times. These appearances, known as *theophanies*, have been recognized ever since the days of the early church as forecasts or anticipations of the incarnation of God the Son as the Son of Man.

Furthermore, the fact that there are *seven* pillars points to Christ as the supreme wisdom of God, since the number seven suggests sufficiency and perfection (as, for example, in the requirement from Proverbs 6:31 [NKJV]: "*He must restore sevenfold.*"). These seven pillars are reminiscent of the seven-fold gifts of the Spirit (see Isaiah 11:2) and of the seven-branched lampstand of the tabernacle of old (see Exodus 25:37), echoed in the seven lampstands of Revelation 1:12. But, as we will see shortly, the seven pillars also point forward to seven vital aspects of the truth that the church proclaims about her Lord.

Also, Christ came to earth to *build a house*, just as Wisdom does in Proverbs. When, at His incarnation, He took on our flesh, it was because He desired to rear for Himself a "house" or "*temple*," as He described His own incarnate body. (See John 2:19.) His apostles later described the church as His body using this same figure of a house. Peter wrote, "*You also, as living stones, are being built up a spiritual house*" (1 Peter 2:5 NKJV). In his epistle to the Ephesians, Paul described how believers in Jesus are "[growing] *into a holy temple in the Lord*" (Ephesians 2:21) and being built into a "*dwelling place of God in the Spirit*" (verse 22); as the God-Man, Jesus Christ Himself is the "*chief cornerstone*" (1 Peter 2:6 NKJV) of this mystic building fitly framed together.

Another association between personified wisdom in Proverbs and the incarnate Christ is found in that fact that within the seven-pillared house that Wisdom built, there was a table furnished with *bread* to eat and *wine* to drink. (See Proverbs 9:2–5.) Hippolytus of the early church commented on this passage in Proverbs:

> Christ furnished His own table, exhibiting His precious and spotless body and blood, which are daily celebrated at that mystic and divine board, being sacrificed in commemoration of that ever-to-be-remembered original table of that mystic and divine supper.

But perhaps the clearest connection between personified wisdom in Proverbs and the incarnate Christ of the New Testament comes through the symbol of the *pillar*. We may be familiar with the expression "a pillar of the church," which is used to describe an individual on whom a local body depends for leadership, guidance, and moral example. This is actually a biblical expression. Paul used it to describe the chief apostles at Jerusalem (James, Cephas [Peter], and John) in Galatians 2:9, and John depicted the Christian undaunted by persecution as "*a pillar in the temple of…God*" (Revelation 3:12). This became a popular expression early in the life of the church. Irenaeus, for example, used it to describe Attalus of

Lyons, who was martyred for his faith in A.D. 177: "He was always the pillar and support of our church."

The figure has become so widely recognized that, in more recent years, it has been used creatively and even somewhat facetiously. William Lamb, who became the 2nd Viscount Melbourne, is credited with having said, "While I cannot be regarded as a pillar, I must be regarded as a buttress of the church, because I support it from the outside." But those whom the Bible depicts as pillars of the church were on the inside, as an integral part of a building. And by looking at another passage where Paul used this symbol, we can recognize that when he spoke of a "pillar of the church," he did not have only particular, faithful, sacrificial saints in mind, but all who are saints in Christ Jesus. When we consider this other passage, we will also see more clearly the connection to personified wisdom.

In his first letter to Timothy, Paul said that *"the household of God, which is the church of the living God,"* is *"the pillar and bulwark of the truth"* (1 Timothy 3:15). Here, he was speaking not so much of an individual as the church's pillar, but rather of the church itself as a pillar. But what is the truth that it upholds?

Paul said immediately afterward, *"Great indeed, we confess, is the mystery of our religion: [God] was manifested in the flesh..."* (1 Timothy 3:16). The word translated *"indeed"* here (*kai* in Greek), which introduces Paul's magnificent authentication of the incarnation, is like a hand linking together the phrases *"the church of the living God"* and *"[God] was manifested in the flesh,"* making them one. As *Ellicott's Commentary on the Whole Bible* expresses it, this word *kai*...

> ...is not simply copulative [adding one phrase to another], but heightens the force of the prediction. Yes, confessedly great is the mystery—for the glorious truth which the church of God pillar-like upholds is none other than that stupendous mystery, in other ages not made known but then revealed—the mystery of Christ, in all His loving manifestations and glorious triumph. Yes, confessedly great—so great that the massive grandeur of the pillar is only in proportion to the truth it supports.

In this passage, Paul actually called the church both the pillar and the bulwark of the truth. This latter term has been rendered various ways in English translations: "foundation," "support," "main-stay," even "basement." But, however the term is translated, the meaning is that the unique foundational truth upon which the church rests, and which she in turn upholds, is that of the manifestation of God in the flesh. The true church is built upon Him who was born, lived, and died as the God-Man. That the Son of God became the Son of Man was one of the glorious truths given among the many things surely believed by the early church. The church today must not forget that this is the mighty, glorious message that alone can heal the open sores of the world's sins and sorrows: "He who was rich for our sakes became poor, so that we through His poverty might be made rich." (See 2 Corinthians 8:9.) If this foundation or bulwark is destroyed, then what can the righteous and unrighteous do? (See Psalm 11:3.)

The early church was so dynamic in its witness because it continued stead-fastly in this particular aspect of the Christian faith. And in our day, all who are *"living stones,"* built into the *"spiritual house"* (1 Peter 2:5) and endowed with wisdom, are under the obligation of crying out *"upon the highest places of the city"* (Proverbs 9:3 KJV) that Jesus became a partaker of flesh and blood (see Hebrews 2:14–18) in order *"to seek and to save that which was lost"* (Luke 19:10). We are not to content ourselves with sitting at the door doing nothing. (See Proverbs 9:14.) Did not the same Solomon leave it on record that *"he that winneth souls is wise"* (Proverbs 11:30 KJV), revealing Him who is *Wisdom* in the winning of them?

It is of great interest that, in 1 Timothy 3:16, Paul presented in seven parts (when his introduction is included) the truth that the church, pillar-like, upholds:

+ Great is the mystery of our religion
+ God was manifested in the flesh
+ Vindicated in the Spirit
+ Seen by angels
+ Preached among the nations
+ Believed on in the world
+ Taken up in glory

This is an epitome of the church's proclamation of its incarnate, crucified, and risen Lord. Many interpreters believe that Paul has preserved here a frag-ment of some Christian hymn or creed. (He did this in at least five other places in the Pastoral Epistles, where he introduced quotations with the expression *"The saying is sure."*) All those who would be wise to the winning of souls, and wise to the salvation and growth of their own souls, would do well to meditate on each of the seven truths presented here, and that is what we will do in the pages that follow. We will discover that these seven facets of the church's proclamation of its Lord embody seven vital doctrinal pillars that are foundational for our understanding of God and our growth in wisdom and knowledge. One chapter of this book will be devoted to each of these pillars:

1. The Pillar of Mystery
2. The Pillar of Incarnation
3. The Pillar of Vindication
4. The Pillar of Revelation
5. The Pillar of Proclamation
6. The Pillar of Belief
7. The Pillar of Glorification

The Man Christ Jesus is the only hope of emancipation from the bondage of sin and eternal doom. When we meditate reverently on the events and truths of His coming to earth, we appreciate more deeply the great salvation that we have received, and we become more eager to share these liberating truths with others. Let us, then, examine and reflect upon each of these statements that Paul made about the incarnate Christ and that the church, like a pillar, upholds.

1

THE PILLAR OF MYSTERY

"Great indeed, we confess, is the mystery of our religion."
—1 Timothy 3:16

The introduction that Paul gave to his unique summary of the incarnation of Christ—*"Great indeed, we confess, is the mystery of our religion"*—emphasized the validity of the virgin birth, that great mystery of the faith. It is, of course, possible to understand the word *"mystery"* here as referring instead to what follows, that is, to the mystery of the whole progress of Christ's incarnation, earthly life, proclamation, and ascension. But the virgin birth is so essential to the redemption and regeneration of humanity that we have every reason to believe Paul would introduce his epitome of the church's proclamation about its Lord with a reference to the wonderful divine act that was necessary to effect human salvation through the coming of Jesus.

THE "MYSTERY" OF OUR FAITH

How gifted by the Spirit Paul was in expressing truth in such fitting and arresting language! Among the mysteries mentioned in Scripture, the particular one the apostle dealt with in the passage before us must surely be the deepest of them all. It is *"the mystery,"* or "mystic secret," of our faith that he referred to when he said earlier in 1 Timothy 3 that church leaders must *"hold the mystery of the faith with a clear conscience"* (verse 9).

It is profitable to compare some of the ways that Paul's statement *"Great indeed, we confess, is the mystery of our religion"* has been translated:

+ "Beyond dispute, grand is that mystic secret, as set forth in our confession-chant."

+ "Without controversy great is the mystery of godliness."

+ "Great beyond question is the mystery of our religion."

+ "This religion of ours is a tremendous mystery."

+ "The hidden truth of godliness is great."

How strikingly emphatic is this assertion, implying, as it does, that there can be no question about the validity of the truth, namely, that Jesus was God manifested in the flesh, and that, because of its genuineness and truthfulness, it is entitled to full acceptance by faith. The mystery of how God could assume our created nature may be beyond our finite comprehension, but this greatest event in human history itself is beyond all dispute or doubt.

Prophets and apostles, by common consent, accepted the virgin birth as the basis of the Christian faith. Under the inspiration of the Spirit, hundreds of years before Christ was born, Isaiah predicted, *"The Lord himself shall give you a sign; Behold, a virgin shall conceive, and bear a son, and shall call his name Immanuel"* (Isaiah 7:14 KJV). John opened his gospel with statements affirming his agreement with the historicity of the incarnation of his Lord, including, *"The Word became flesh and dwelt among us"* (John 1:14). The incarnate Christ Himself declared, *"Abraham rejoiced to see my day: and he saw it* [the preexistent One in the flesh] *and was glad"* (John 8:56 KJV). This basis of our faith is further authenticated by all the apostles, principally by Paul. With boldness he made it plain, in the passage that is the subject of our meditation in this book, that he accepted, without any demur or apology, the glorious revelation that the Babe of Bethlehem was God manifested in the flesh and that His incarnation was vindicated by the Holy Spirit and by angels.

There is, moreover, the apostle's remarkable testimony to Christ's humility, as well as to the fact of the incarnation, in his marvelous description of Jesus being equal with God and yet assuming the form of a slave, being born in human likeness. (See Philippians 2:6–8.) Jesus became the *outward-fashion* of God for all to see. *"I came down from heaven"* (John 6:38), Christ affirmed, and voluntarily assumed our humanity so that He might die as the sinless Substitute for sinners. To this authoritative statement we can add the further New Testament language of Christ becoming a partaker of our flesh and blood in order to destroy the power of the devil. (See Hebrews 2:14–18.) Rich in glory, He became poor on earth, so that all who are saved by His grace and power might, through His earthly poverty, become enriched by His mercy. (See 2 Corinthians 8:9.)

Many have stumbled over the question of the virgin birth simply because they have tried to explain it by human reasoning, but such a question baffles explanation. And so our position to all adverse criticism must be, certainly in light of the prophetic and apostolic testimony we have just reviewed: Well! Here is a scriptural fact! We cannot fully understand it, but we accept and believe it!

It is an essential pillar of wisdom to submit reverently to the presence of mystery. When we do this in the case of our Lord's virgin birth, we are led to consider that although the revealed truth of such a fact may be contrary to human reason, yet to the believer it is faith, and not reason, that must of necessity operate. Reason would say, "Christ born of a virgin! Impossible!" The virgin birth an impossibility? So may reason declare; but faith, growing in wisdom, learns to accept the angel's word, *"With God nothing will be impossible"* (Luke 1:37), even as Mary had to when her reason failed to comprehend the truth. Yes, and faith delights to respond, even as Mary did, *"Let it be…according to your word"* (Luke 1:38). In the words of the old poem by Joseph Juste Scaliger:

> Seek not the cause, for 'tis not in thy reach,
> Of all the truths prophetic volumes teach,
> Those "secret things" imparted from on high,
> Which speak at once, and veil the Deity.
> Pass on; nor rash explore the depths that lie
> Divinely hid in sacred mystery.[1]

Indeed, it is necessary to possess a virgin life if the mystery of our Lord's virgin birth is to be rightly appreciated. By this we mean that a person cannot fully understand the revealed facts of this holy mystery unless that person's life is made and kept holy by the same blessed Holy Spirit who carried out the wondrous conception of our Savior's human body.

In fact, one wonders if any particular part of our Lord's person and work can be rightly understood unless there is a corresponding spiritual experience. For

1. Henry Southgate, *Suggestive Thoughts on Religious Subjects: A Dictionary of Quotations and Select Passages* (London: Charles Griffin & Company, 1881), 193.

instance, how can we grasp the tremendous miracle of our Lord's birth unless, first of all, we have been born again by the same Holy One who made Christ's birth possible?

Or how can we follow the Master's footsteps as He trod the streets of Galilee and other parts, living a holy, sinless life amid the pollutions of earth, "the lily among thorns," unless we ourselves are seeking to live lives of detachment, even as He did, from the ways and pursuits of this world?

Or how can we enter rightly into the sorrow of His rejection by His own people, or the persecution of His friends and foes alike, or His tragic betrayal by a professed disciple, unless, in some measure, we have had to tread the same thorn-strewn road and receive many wounds without cause?

Or how can we linger under the shadow of Gethsemane's olive trees and penetrate the meaning and mystery of His soul agony as He cries, "*Not my will, but thine, be done*" (Luke 22:42), unless we have come to some Gethsemane of surrender of our own and learned to say, as He said, "*Shall I not drink the cup which the Father has given me?*" (John 18:11).

Or how can we grasp the significance of His cross as He dies, unless we ourselves have come to the place of death, even to the place called Calvary, that is, "a skull," suggesting nothingness, emptiness, and death?

Or how can we realize the truth of His glorious resurrection, unless we are walking in "*newness of life*" (Romans 6:4)?

You see the thought! The apprehension of the truth concerning Christ requires a spiritual correspondence. In other words, to know Christ, we must live Christ! And so, we return to our opening word, namely, that the virgin birth of our Lord can be profitably meditated upon only by men and women whose lives are virgin. Paul made it clear that "*the natural man does not receive the things of the Spirit of God, for they are foolishness to him; nor can he know them, because they are spiritually discerned*" (1 Corinthians 2:14 NKJV). This dictum is certainly true in respect to the things of the Spirit of God in connection with the conception of Jesus in the Virgin's womb.

Now, it is with the feeling of hesitation that one approaches this solemn, holy mystery of our Lord's entrance into our world as a human babe. The theme is so vast and delicate, so profound and incomprehensible, that one trembles lest one word should be expressed that misrepresents in the least degree such a wonderful revelation.

May the same Holy Spirit who overshadowed Mary as she conceived her Son overshadow our hearts and minds as we seek to set forth the revealed truths regarding the mystery of godliness: God manifested in the flesh! We readily confess there is no other theme centering on the person of our Lord in which one realizes how necessary it is to give heed to Solomon's advice in respect to "*find*[ing] *out acceptable words*" (Ecclesiastes 12:10 KJV) than that of the Savior being "conceived by the Holy Spirit, born of the Virgin Mary" (in the words of the Apostles' Creed). Such a truth is both deep and delicate, infinite and incomprehensible, so that unless the mind is overshadowed by the Holy Spirit, no progress in the study of such a foundational revelation can be made. "*Put off your shoes from your feet, for the place on which you are standing is holy ground*" (Exodus 3:5).

CLEARING AWAY THE "MIST"

Before we come to the main teaching about our subject, it may be fitting to clear the ground, so to speak. Although the virgin birth is in many respects a mystery, and will ever remain so, yet there is a good deal of so-called mystery that is nothing else but "mist." Now mist is not mystery and can therefore be penetrated and cleared away! Often the mist of vague, partial, mistaken notions, leading to half-truths, surrounds the fact of our Lord's virgin birth, thereby making the mystery itself needlessly greater. And so, as one can rise above the natural mist by climbing a hill or mountain, so by the aid of the Holy Spirit, our divine Teacher and Revealer, we can rise above all the false or partial conceptions of this august truth we are considering and comprehend simply and fully all that we ought to. We will seek to dispel much of the mist surrounding this mystery in the course of this chapter. The same Holy Spirit who conceived our Lord is perfectly willing to take of this matter that belongs to Christ and show it unto us! (See John 16:13–14.)

It may help to clear away some of the unnecessary mist that has gathered around this sublime, sacred mystery of the virgin birth of our Lord, if we give a somewhat brief consideration to the terms, scriptural and otherwise, that are often used to denote it.

We may consider first the phrase *Immaculate Conception*. This term is often incorrectly applied to the virgin birth, which constitutes a manifest blunder that confuses one idea with another. This term was used for the first time in a Papal Bull entitled *Ineffabilis Deus*, which was promulgated by Pope Pius IX on December 8, 1854. In this Roman Catholic dogma, the central proclamation is that "the blessed Virgin Mary was from the first instant of her conception"—that is, her own conception—"by a singular grace and privilege of Almighty God, in view of the merits of Christ Jesus, the Savior of man, preserved free from all stain of original sin." This doctrine was promulgated to give Mary, or the Mother of God, as the Catholic Church calls her, a more exalted place by lifting her out of the realm of ordinary human beings. Whatever we might think of this teaching, we must recognize that the phrase "Immaculate Conception" does not refer to our Lord's birth but to the idea of Mary's sinlessness from the moment when she was conceived within her own mother's womb. So we should not apply the phrase to the circumstances of Jesus' birth.

Another term connected with the birth of Jesus is *incarnation*. Although this is not a scriptural word, it is one we often employ in connection with the virgin birth of our Lord. The word *incarnate* means "to embody in flesh." And this is what really happened in Mary's child: "*The Word became flesh*" (John 1:14); "*[God] was manifested in the flesh*" (1 Timothy 3:16). Charles Wesley wrote of the virgin birth and the incarnation closely together in his beloved Christmas carol "Hark! the Herald Angels Sing":

> Late in time behold Him come,
> Offspring of a virgin's womb.
> Veiled in flesh the God-head see,
> Hail th'incarnate Deity!
> Pleased as man with men to dwell,
> Jesus our Emmanuel.

Nevertheless, we must recognize that *incarnation* is a broad word and that it is identified not only with our Lord's entrance into our world as a babe but also with His whole life from His birth forward. Throughout the days of His flesh, He was the Incarnate One—yes, and He still is, for in glory He possesses the human form that He died and rose with, although it is now glorified. He is still "*this same Jesus*" (Acts 1:11 kjv). And the wonder in heaven now, and forever, is the presence of Him who is the God-Man. The incarnation of Jesus will be the theme of our next chapter.

The virgin birth of Jesus is sometimes also referred to as a *supernatural birth* or a *miraculous birth*. Even this designation, although an oft-quoted one, will not do, unless we fully understand what we mean when we use it. The *birth* of our Lord was not itself supernatural or miraculous. By this we mean there is no intimation that the process of birth was in any way exceptional. Mary's child was formed within her womb and then born in just the same natural way as the child of Elizabeth, Mary's cousin. Perfectly natural phenomena are suggested by the speaker in a Messianic psalm: *"Thou art he who took me from the womb; thou didst keep me safe upon my mother's breasts. Upon thee was I cast from my birth, and since my mother bore me thou has been my God"* (Psalm 22:9–10). As Malcolm Muggeridge has observed:

> If God chose to become incarnate as Jesus, then His birth, whatever marvels may have accompanied it, must have had the same characteristics as any other; just as, on the cross, the suffering of the man into whom the Bethlehem child grew must have been of the same nature as that of the two delinquents crucified beside Him. Otherwise, Jesus's humanity would have been a fraud; in which case, His divinity would have been fraudulent, too. The perfection of Jesus's divinity was expressed in the perfection of His humanity, and vice versa. He was God because He was so sublimely a man, and Man because, in all His sayings and doings, in the grace of His Person and Words, in the love and compassion that shone out of Him, He walked so closely with God. As Man alone, Jesus could not have saved us; as God alone, he would not; Incarnate, He could and did.[2]

The miraculous element was not in the formation of our Lord's body but in the manner of its begetting. The birth of our Lord is supernatural only in that He was conceived by a virgin, that is, apart from the ordinary course of nature. It is in this regard that we can view both Mary and Elizabeth's conceptions as miraculous. The birth of John the Baptist was miraculous in that Elizabeth, his mother, had traveled beyond the age when, through the ordinary course of nature, it was possible to conceive and bear. The birth of our Lord was even more miraculous in that Mary bore Him as a result of a divine creative act, apart from human generation. A. T. Scofield has observed that both births were supernatural: that to Elizabeth was because it was *too late*, that to Mary because it was *too soon*. But what we really have in view is a miraculous or supernatural conception, not specifically a birth.

So we must agree with Dr. Sweet that the only term that is sufficiently specific is *virgin birth*, inasmuch as according to the New Testament statement Mary

---

2. Malcolm Muggeridge, *Jesus: The Man Who Lives* (San Francisco: Harper and Row, 1975), 30.

was at the time of this birth *virgo intacto*.[3] But not only is virgin birth a title "sufficiently specific," it is the only scriptural way of describing how God brought Jesus into the world through Mary, and it is, therefore, the most correct term. It specifies that Mary was a virgin when she conceived Jesus and still a virgin when she gave birth to Him.

THE FACT OF THE VIRGIN BIRTH

It is under this term that we will now summarize what can be taught clearly about the virgin birth of Jesus, still with the purpose of dispelling mist so that we can appreciate mystery.

There are two Scripture passages that supply the *fact* of our Lord's virgin birth. The prediction of it is in Isaiah 7:14: "*Behold, a virgin shall conceive, and bear a son, and shall call his name Immanuel*" (KJV). The fulfillment of it is in Matthew 1:22–23: "*All this took place to fulfil what the Lord had spoken by the prophet: 'Behold, a virgin shall conceive and bear a son, and his name shall be called Emmanuel.*'"

Arising out of these statements are several questions that demand our study and attention. First, what is meant specifically by the Hebrew and Greek words translated as "*virgin*" in these passages? There are actually two different meanings. In Isaiah, the Hebrew term is *'almah*, which denotes any young woman of marriageable age. And so Isaiah's statement could originally have been understood to mean that a woman who was then an *'almah* would conceive and bear a child with her husband after she was married. The true circumstances of Jesus' birth are communicated more exactly through the Greek term used in Matthew, *parthenos*, which signifies a woman who is able to say, like Mary, "*I know not a man*" (Luke 1:34 KJV)—that is, one who has never had sexual relations. The scholars who created the Septuagint translation of the Old Testament into Greek in the centuries before Jesus used the word *parthenos* to translate *'almah* in Isaiah, thus conveying the meaning that allowed Matthew to recognize Jesus' conception as a fulfillment of Isaiah's prophecy.

So, the logical conclusion is that Mary, as a virgin, was a "young unmarried woman who had preserved the purity of her body," as Cruden's concordance defines the term.[4] As we noted just above, Mary remained a virgin until after Christ was born, as Scripture clearly teaches in Matthew 1:25, which says that Joseph married her but "*knew her not until she had borne a son.*" Thereafter she

---

3. Louis Matthews Sweet, *The Birth and Infancy of Jesus Christ* (London: Cassell, 1907).
4. Alexander Cruden, *A Complete Concordance to the Holy Scriptures of the Old and New Testaments* (Philadelphia: Kimber, Conrad and Co., 1906), 780.

lived in the usual relations of wedlock with Joseph and had at least four sons and two daughters with him. (See Matthew 13:55–56.)

Another question that these scriptural passages raise is, "Why was Christ born of a virgin?" This question is not so easily answered as the other. But Thomas Watson suggested three reasons when he discussed "Christ's Humiliation in His Incarnation" in his *Body of Divinity*.[5]

First, *for decency*. "It became not God to have any mother but a maid," he wrote, "and it became not a maid to have any other son but a God."

Second, *for necessity*. If our Lord had been born according to the laws of natural procreation, He would have been defiled. If He had had a human father, as well as a human mother, then with the psalmist He would have had to cry, "*Behold, I was brought forth in iniquity, and in sin did my mother conceive me*" (Psalm 51:5). All who are born after the ordinary course of nature have the tincture of sin within. But Christ was to be absolutely sinless—"*holy, blameless, unstained, separated from sinners*" (Hebrews 7:26). His substance had to be pure and immaculate; otherwise, His right to redeem would be forfeited. Hence, He must be virgin-born! In the formation of His body, there had to be no original sin, so that He could commence where Adam did; thus, in Him there was not the mixture of human seed. Well we might say:

> Approach, thou gentle Little One,
> Of stainless Mother born to earth,
> Free from all wedded union,
> The MEDIATOR's twofold birth.
>
> What joys to the vast universe
> In that chaste Maiden's womb are borne;
> Ages set free from sorrow's curse
> Spring forth, and everlasting morn.[6]

Third, *to answer to the type*. "Melchizedek was a type of Christ, who is said to be '*without father and mother*' [Hebrews 7:3]. Christ, being born of a virgin, answered the type; he was without father and without mother; without mother as he was God, without father" as He was born of a virgin.

---

5. Thomas Watson, *A Body of Practical Divinity* (Aberdeen: George King, 1838), 178.
6. M. Aurelius Clemens Prudentius, *The Nativity of Jesus Christ*, quoted in Southgate, *Suggestive Thoughts on Religious Subjects*, 195.

Yet another question that has doubtless troubled some minds in light of the scriptural teaching is as follows. The Bible asks, *"How can he who is born of woman be clean?"* (Job 25:4). How then could Christ be born of a woman, even if she were a virgin, and yet be without sin? In other words, Christ, we declare, was made of the flesh and blood of a virgin; and since the purest virgin is stained with original sin, how could our Lord be without sin? The Catholic Church, as we noted above, seeks to address this concern through the doctrine of Mary's "Immaculate Conception." But there is a straightforward answer to it in the Scriptures. This seemingly difficult knot is untied for us in Luke 1:35, where Gabriel said to Mary, *"The Holy Spirit will come upon you, and the power of the Most High will overshadow you; therefore the child to be born will be called holy, the Son of God."*

Mark the phrase *"The Holy Spirit will come upon you"* (or *"overshadow you"*), for it means that

> the Holy Ghost did consecrate and purify that part of the virgin's flesh whereof Christ was made. As the alchemist extracts and draws away the dross from the gold, so the Holy Ghost refines and clarifies that part of the virgin's flesh, separating it from sin. Though the Virgin Mary herself had sin, yet that part of her flesh, whereof Christ was made, was without sin; otherwise it must have been an impure conception.

The Bible also lets us see the birth of our Lord from its divine side, just as the prediction about the virgin birth and its fulfillment let us see it from the human side. The angel of the Lord, in banishing Joseph's doubts about Mary's purity and morality, announced, *"That which is conceived in her is of the Holy Spirit"* (Matthew 1:20). Professor James Orr remarked in his article in *The Fundamentals* on "The Virgin Birth of Christ": "There is another factor—'conceived by the Holy Spirit.' What happened was a divine, created miracle wrought in the production of this new humanity which secured from its earliest germinal beginnings freedom from the slightest taint of sin."[7] From both of these perspectives, we can understand how Jesus could be born of a woman and still be entirely free from sin.

And so Paul declared, *"When the time had fully come, God sent forth his Son, born of woman, born under the law"* (Galatians 4:4). Such a phrase describes the perfect humanity of our Lord and gives us His wondrous birth from the human

---

7. James Orr, "The Virgin Birth of Christ," in *The Fundamentals: A Testimony to the Truth* (Chicago: Testimony Publishing Company, 1910), 18.

standpoint. But one may ask a further question: "Why was Christ born of a woman?" Well, there are one or two answers to such a question.

First, it is *a fulfillment of a promise.* The great redemption promise of Genesis 3:15 was that the seed of the woman would break the serpent's head. Woman, who was made a sinner by the serpent, would produce One who would destroy the serpent's power. Some scholars find an allusion to the promise of Genesis 3:15 in 1 Timothy 2:15: *"She shall be saved through the child bearing"* (RV). It is evident that woman is saved from her sin through the Child born of the woman, even Mary, who is highly favored among women.

Second, it is also *a removal of reproach.* By being born of a woman, Christ has rolled away the reproach from woman, which became hers by the seduction of the serpent. In taking her flesh, our Lord honors her sex and thereby unties the knot of Eve's disobedience. The writers of the early church, we are told, often pressed this analogy between Eve and Mary in language similar to this: "As at the first the woman had made man a sinner, so now, to make him amends, she brings him a Savior."

Of course, none of us should imagine that we can fully explain or understand the mystery of the virgin birth, even after as much of the mist as possible has been dispelled. No matter what light we may receive, the mystery of the God-Man in one Person remains. Bishop Handley Moule asserted that "in Scripture a mystery may be a fact which, when revealed, we cannot understand in detail, though we can know it, and act upon it....It is a thing only to be known when revealed."[8] And in reference to the virgin birth, it is certainly true that "we cannot understand it in detail, though we can know it, and act upon it." In the presence of such a holy miracle, "there can be no fitting attitude," to use the words of Dr. Morgan, "of the human intellect save that of acceptance of the truth, without any attempt to explain the absolute mystery." This, as we have said, is a first pillar of wisdom: to accept mystery without attempting to explain it.

Truly, Paul was right when he declared that the mystery of our religion is *"great indeed."* Yes, this mystery is great, too great for our finite minds to comprehend! Mystery! Why, who can unravel this?

Behold here a sacred riddle or paradox—"God manifest in the flesh." That man should be made in God's image was a wonder, but that God should be made in man's image is a greater wonder. That the Ancient of Days should

---

8. Handley Carr Glyn Moule, *The Epistle to the Ephesians* (Cambridge: University Press, 1893), 50.

be born, that he who thunders in the heavens should cry in the cradle…; that he who rules the stars should suck the breast; that a virgin should conceive; that Christ should be made of a woman, and of that woman which himself made; that the branch should bear the vine; that the mother should be younger than the child she bare, and the child in the womb bigger than the mother; that the human nature should not be God, yet one with God…. Christ taking flesh is a mystery we shall never fully understand till we come to heaven, when our light shall be clear, as well as our love perfect.[9]

No wonder a divine of old said, "I can scarce get past His cradle in my wondering to wonder at His cross. The infant Jesus is, in some views, a greater marvel than Jesus with the purple robe and the crown of thorns!"

Fathom the mystery! Never! We can only bow before it in holy wonder and marvel at the greatness of the God who could make such a wondrous birth as our Savior's possible. Let us take heed, lest we rush in where angels fear to tread. Rather, let our attitude be one of wisdom, as depicted here:

I will seek to believe rather than to reason, to adore rather than to explain, to give thanks rather than to penetrate, to love rather than to know, to humble myself rather than to speak.[10]

CONTROVERSIES OVER THE VIRGIN BIRTH

And so, in this spirit, we come to the main teaching about our subject. Earlier in this chapter we noted some of the ways in which Paul's introduction to his epitome of the church's proclamation about Christ—"*Great indeed, we confess, is the mystery of our religion*"—has been translated. The phrase "*we confess*" actually represents a single adverb in Greek, *homologoumenos*, meaning "confessedly," that is, "admittedly." This term has been translated in various ways: "beyond dispute," "no one would deny," "beyond all question," "by common confession." Behind each translation is the idea of a united confession; this is certainly implied in the Greek word *homologoumenos*, which signifies "by consent of all." The King James Version appropriately translates this term as "*without controversy*."

---

9. Thomas Watson, "Christ's Humiliation in His Incarnation," in *A Body of Divinity: Contained in Sermons upon the Westminster Catechism's Assembly*, 1692.
10. Quesnel, "Le nouveau testament, avec des reflexions morales sur chaque verset," translated and quoted in Edward Meyrick Goulburn, *Thoughts upon the Liturgical Gospels*, vol. 1 (London: Rivingtons, 1886), 105.

It is highly ironic, therefore, how much controversy there has been about the virgin birth! Although substantiated throughout Scripture as an undisputed fact, no other part of the Christian doctrine has been so keenly assailed as the subject of our Lord's virgin birth. One trembles when one comes to examine the criticisms leveled at it, because they not only seek the destruction of the miraculous, and of the very foundation of our gospel revelation, but such unworthy and unwarranted criticisms shamefully dishonor our blessed, adorable Lord. For the help of believers, we offer the following summary and refutation of these criticisms, trusting that it will help many to strengthen their faith in this wonderful means by which Jesus came to earth.

From the earliest days of the Christian church, the virgin birth has been bitterly opposed by various schools of learning and religious thought. The *Ebionites*, for example, were a particular sect of early Jewish believers who were not regarded as part of the true church because they held that the Mosaic law was binding on Christians, they denied the apostolate of Paul, and they rejected the virgin birth. Because of these three important matters, they remained outside the recognized Christian church until their sect disappeared around the end of the fourth century.

These Ebionites possessed a gospel based on Matthew's, but from which the story of the virgin birth was absent. Yet such was a spurious copy, a mutilated and corrupted form of Matthew's gospel. Because they used it, the Ebionites held that Jesus was a man, naturally born, and not the "offspring of a virgin's womb." They recognized, of course, that He was above the ordinary man in that He resembled the Spirit-led man or prophet of Old Testament times. But even with such endowments, they thought He was still a mere man who sprang from human parents. (Such a view has passed into the thinking of many today, for "the Ebionite being dead, yet speaketh.")

The *Gnostics* were another early sect. They, or at least their forerunners, were prevalent in Paul's day and are possibly referred to in Colossians 2:18–19, where Paul tried to warn the believers at Colossae against mystical heresies. The word *Gnostic* comes from the Greek word *gnostikos*, which means "good at knowing." And so these Gnostics were the "know-it-alls" of Paul's day; that is, they presumed to know after the order of a "fleshy mind" more than the revealed truth of God, such as the apostle was declaring.

In respect to Christ, they allegorized away His person and work. They held that He possessed two forms—one called Jesus, born in a natural way, and another called Christ, which came upon Him at His baptism and which indwelled Jesus until just before the cross, when the Christ part went back to heaven, and the Jesus part that was left died upon the cross. Keeping this teaching in mind, one is enabled to understand the epistle to the Colossians more clearly, since Paul's purpose in writing it was to counteract this error of false mysticism. In a masterly way, the apostle showed that our Lord "is not two Beings (Jesus and Christ) somehow united, nor two persons with two minds, two wills, two conflicting existences, wedded in impossible bonds; but one being, harmonious, symmetrical, consistent—not God in man, or God and man, but the God-Man."[11] Would that we could hear the apostle's warning of Colossians 2:8, "*See to it that no one makes a prey of you by philosophy and empty deceit,*" more often than we do!

Coming to present-day criticisms and theories, one is appalled to find how generally the virgin birth of our Lord is denied. It is openly declared from the professor's chair, as well as from the church pulpit, that your Savior and mine did not come into the world as the Bible says He did, but that He was a man, just as other men, and that in respect to His conception, there was nothing miraculous. Professor Orr said it would be a perilous day for the church when, in obedience to the demand of so-called "modern thought," the belief in the virgin birth was parted with. He did not believe that, in really faithful circles, that day would ever come. Ah, but apostasy is rapidly spreading; and since Professor Orr's day, many in the church have yielded to the demands of so-called "modern thought" and have parted with their faith in the virgin birth.

The "Non-miraculous" Criticisms

Now, in order that we might be able to meet the modern skeptical view regarding the virgin birth and, at the same time, confirm our faith, let us classify the objections raised. There are, first of all, the "non-miraculous" criticisms. The trend of modern thought is to deny everything supernatural and explain all that appears to be of a miraculous nature in the Bible from a natural standpoint. By the process of human reason, the seemingly inexplicable matters are explained as natural phenomena. And so the finding of Professor Orr is perfectly true in this respect, that the chief cause for the denial of the virgin birth of our Lord is the rise and rapid spread of a school of historical criticism that aims at the complete expurgation of the miraculous element from the life of our Lord all through. Such a method of

11. Arthur Tappan Pierson, *"Many Infallible Proofs": The Evidences of Christianity* (New York: Fleming H. Revell Company, 1886), 239.

attack is, to say the least, satanic, for it weakens the fact of God's omnipotence and also refuses the reliable testimony of the New Testament writers.

The sum of the teaching of this particular school is that of the Ebionites, namely, that Christ was an ordinary man after the natural order. The argument goes that since the Creator has decreed that the production of a child can come only by human contact, it is, therefore, impossible for Him to break that law. But the simple answer of faith is: *"With God nothing will be impossible"* (Luke 1:37). He is the Lord of all law, as well as the Lord of all life!

The "Documentary Defects" Objection

Other critics claim that the virgin birth must be rejected on the grounds of a lack of evidence. We may call this the "documentary defects" objection. Now, since there is no adequate reason why any intelligent believer should have any uncertainty as to the verity of this most important fact of our religion, even though its references are meager in New Testament documents, let us take this objection of documentary deficiency upon its own ground. First, let us consider the reliability of the evidence.

Perhaps, by way of introduction, we may be allowed to quote from a product of the so-called "Higher Criticism," namely, Peake's *Commentary.* In it, we read: "As regards the birth stories of Matthew and Luke, we find ourselves in doubt on many points, and there is reason to believe that a reverent imagination has been at work on traditional material."[12] Now, this is a very serious allegation; and if true, it destroys the validity of the Scriptures, which have been inspired by God. The questions before us, then, are these: Can we rely upon the Gospels as being genuine productions? Or are they merely the product of "reverent imagination" woven together out of "traditional material"?

Such a question is important, because if the contention of the higher critics is proven, then the writers of the New Testament records were guilty of falsification and gross deception. Well, on turning to the Gospels themselves, what do we find? Why, that Matthew and Luke are the only two who give us any account of our Lord's birth and infancy and that their united testimony is that He was conceived of the Holy Spirit and born of the Virgin Mary.

Let us try to prove the orthodox position. First, these two gospels are genuine documents of the Apostolic Age. There is abundant evidence that the

---

12. Arthur Samuel Peake, ed., *A Commentary on the Bible* (London: T. C. & E. C. Jack, 1920), 14.

early disciples treated Matthew and Luke as genuine documents. For instance, Professor William Sanday considers them to be the oldest and most obviously authentic parts of the New Testament.[13] Their evidence may therefore be accepted without reservation.

Next, the virgin birth narratives are genuine parts of these gospels. In the oldest manuscripts and versions we have of Matthew and Luke, even though some of these are mutilated in parts, the chapters that recount the virgin birth are still to be found. And yet, some of the critics discredit the genuineness of these parts. The chief source of their information is a German critic named Wellhausen, who issued an edition of the Gospels "translated and explained," from which he dropped out entirely the story of the virgin birth, giving no note or explanation of his omissions. Why, such a treatment would be unallowable for anyone dealing with any classical work!

And finally, the very texts have come down to us in their integrity. Here, said Professor Orr in his monumental work on the virgin birth, whom I am following closely under these critical theories, we encounter a new line of attack. The narrative of Luke is a genuine part of the gospel, but have we the text in its original form? The evidence of manuscripts and versions is again decisive. Apart from a few various readings, such as occur in all texts (the chief of them may be seen in the margin of the Revised Version), the chapters in Luke are vouched for as coming down to us in their integrity.

But this evidence does not satisfy some of the critics, and so they set out to delete from the narratives in this way: "Leave out, for example, verses 34 and 35 of chapter 1," that is, Mary's question, *"How shall this be?"* and the angel's answer, which is the crucial verse, *"The Holy Spirit will come upon you,"* and so forth. Cut out or change a few other clauses, and the story of the virgin birth disappears. You have simply the promise of a son, as in the cases of Isaac, Samson, Samuel, and John the Baptist, to be born in the ordinary way, in the estate of marriage. Especially is Luke 1:27, where Mary is twice spoken of as a virgin, to be deleted; and there are some sequential changes. Then, said Harnack, "After these few and easy deletions...the narrative is smooth and nowhere pre-supposes the virgin birth." But Professor Orr countered: "Even then [the] trouble is not over, for...if these deletions are made, one would expect to find some notice of a marriage of Joseph and Mary."[14]

13. See, for example, William Sanday, *Criticism of the New Testament* (New York: Scribner's, 1902), 14.
14. James Orr, *The Virgin Birth of Christ* (New York: Scribner's, 1907), 55.

The "Contradiction of the Evidence" Objection

Another objection raised is the supposed contradiction of the evidence. Matthew and Luke appear to contradict each other in many features; some claim that such contradiction discredits the truth of the virgin birth. Let us turn again to Professor Orr. What had he to say to such an objection?

First, that the narratives are independent of each other. Matthew does not copy from Luke, nor Luke from Matthew, nor both from a common source. That is evident from the whole structure of the narratives and from the so-called discrepancies.

Next, that the narratives are nevertheless related to each other. Now, all the difficulties raised by the critics immediately disappear when we remember that Matthew and Luke gave their accounts of the virgin birth from different standpoints. Take Matthew: In his gospel, he gave us the standpoint of Joseph, and so we have hardly any reference to Mary. Matthew told the outward, or public, experiences that followed the facts that came to Joseph's knowledge; and this account, it will be found, is in dramatic contrast to Luke's version. There is:

+ Joseph's perplexity and suspicions (Matthew 1:19)

+ His thoughts and purposes (Matthew 1:20)

+ His difficulties removed by a divine revelation (Matthew 1:20)

+ His gracious, manly, unquestioning response to such (Matthew 1:24–25)

Luke, on the other hand, gave us the standpoint of Mary, and so Joseph is hardly noticed, except as the one to whom Mary was betrothed. As a tender physician, Luke told us the story of the virgin birth from an inward point of view, as only a physician can, and recorded experiences that are deeply personal. And so we have:

+ Mary's call to motherhood (Luke 1:28)

+ Her maidenly fears (Luke 1:29)

+ Her chaste, pure life (Luke 1:34)

+ Her royal submission (Luke 1:38)

+ Her sacred joy (Luke 1:39–56)

+ Her deliverance (Luke 2:5–7)

Now, not only is this relationship observed in the details surrounding the birth of our Lord, but it can also be traced in the two genealogies that are given by Matthew and Luke. It is affirmed that the two genealogies are totally different from each other and bear apparent marks of contradiction. But, here again, the difficulties disappear as quickly as the morning mist when we remember the standpoint of each writer.

There are two genealogies because the descent of Jesus is traced along two distinct lines. As Dr. W. Choritic pointed out, all confusion is banished when we remember that, to begin with, the natural answer is that every man has two genealogies, that of his father and that of his mother; and that, even in our own legal matters, cases might arise in which the production of both was necessary. To this there is something of a similarity in this present instance.

Take Matthew: This first gospel sets out to show the kingly descent of Him who was *"born king of the Jews"* (Matthew 2:2), and so our Lord's royal or legal descent is traced back to King David. In writing for Jewish readers, Matthew realized it was imperative, at the very outset, "to establish Christ's earthly claim to the throne as the successor of King David."

Take Luke, on the other hand: Luke presented Christ as the perfectly human One, the Son of Man, that is, as the One who became the representative Man; and so, in his gospel, he stressed Jesus' human history; and in the genealogy he gave, he proved the natural descent of Christ by traveling back to Adam.

The "Mythical Theories" Criticism

There are others who would have us regard the virgin birth as a late myth that sprang up to account for the impression that the divine character of Jesus made upon His disciples. These are the "mythical theories." Such a course is perfectly understandable, for if one discards the genuineness of the gospel narratives of the virgin birth, then one must seek to explain its existence with such theories.

According to some critics, the virgin birth is a product of Jewish imagination, a myth that sprang up on Jewish soil, arising out of the prophetic passage of Isaiah 7:14. But, unfortunately for this explanation, it can be shown that in Christ's time, this prophecy was not applied by any Jews to the Messiah, for as we saw above, the Hebrew word used in Isaiah (*'almah*) does not specifically mean *virgin*, but rather a young woman of marriageable age. The idea of a virgin birth was not one likely to spring up in a Jewish mind at all. It had no precedent in the Old Testament, where high honor was put on marriage. (See Deuteronomy 22:20–21.) The sons of promise in the Old Testament were all born of marriage.

Because a Jewish origin is therefore so unlikely, other critics describe the virgin birth as the product of Gentile myths. We find newer theories that assert that the early Christians borrowed or imitated pagan myths of sons of the gods and applied them to Jesus. But such theories are contradicted by the fact that until the middle of the second century, the church held itself strictly and uncompromisingly aloof from everything savoring of paganism. It is useless spending time discussing such absurd and shameful explanations for the doctrine of the virgin birth, for it could be easily shown that there is no comparison between the lustful tales of the sons of gods in heathenism, in which there is no real instance of a virgin birth, and the simple, chaste, beautiful narratives of the Christian Gospels. We can afford to leave the matter where Professor Sweet did in his book *The Birth and Infancy of Jesus Christ*: We may with confidence assert that wide excursions into ethnic mythology and folklore have failed to produce a single authentic parallel in fact or in form to the infancy narratives.

THE MYSTERY OF THE VIRGIN BIRTH

Now that we have traveled so far in seeking to prove the fact of the virgin birth, thereby confirming our faith, let us go on reverently to handle the mystical truth that such a sacred theme presents. In doing so, let us remember our opening thought—that the mystery itself cannot be explained. With reverent, adoring hearts, we accept and believe it. So, even as we now seek to appreciate God's wisdom in sending His Son into the world through this means, we will also seek to grow in godly wisdom and rest on the Pillar of Mystery by accepting in faith a divine truth that reason cannot comprehend.

An essential question from the most ancient book in the world is: *"How can he be clean that is born of a woman?"* (Job 25:4 KJV). And the miracle of the virgin birth is that our Lord was absolutely clean, although He was born of a woman. How such a miracle was effected we have already seen—through the overshadowing power of the Holy Spirit. But let us view the matter from another aspect. Look for a moment at the pedigree of Christ in Matthew's genealogy. Four women are mentioned there. Who are they? Tamar, who deceived her father-in-law, Judah, into fathering her child when he denied her his younger son as a new husband in her widowhood. Ruth, who was a woman of great faith, but also a Moabite, a Gentile foreigner. Rahab, who sheltered the Israelite spies and is numbered among the heroes of the faith in Hebrews 11, but who was previously a prostitute. Bathsheba, whom David took in adultery, even though she was married to another man. And this is just to consider the experiences of the women in the genealogy, not to mention the men, who include wicked, idolatrous, murderous kings like Manasseh. From an ancestry so filled with human sinfulness, despite the faith and obedience of so many of the figures, it would have been impossible to have produced one who, like our Lord, possessed a sinless nature, unless some miracle had taken place. And the miracle of the mystery of His birth is that in spite of the sinful pedigree He possessed, through the conception of the Holy Spirit, He came into the world a perfectly sinless person.

And in this, there is an evidence of His peerless grace. He who was the highest stoops to the lowest; He who was so holy makes Himself of no reputation but identifies Himself with sin-stained humanity so that He might go down to the lowest depths of human need and debasement to raise fallen humanity up to purity and back to God.

Let us reverently consider the stupendous mystery that reposes within the heart of the miracle of the virgin birth, like some precious jewel within a box. There are, it would seem, two sides of the mystery.

The Union of Deity and Humanity

There is, first, the combination of deity and humanity. It is a very great wonder indeed to realize that the Holy Spirit framed the body of Christ within the Virgin's body, but the wonder and mystery are intensified when we remember that the Holy Spirit united deity and humanity together. God and man were taken hold of by the Holy Spirit and formed into one person. This is a great mystery, baffling explanation, and one that the angels pry into with adoration. (See 1 Peter 1:12.)

Dr. Handley Moule remarked that "God did not send His Son to join a man born of a woman, which would have been an alliance of two persons, not a harmony of two natures in relation to one person."[15] Oh, beloved, how incomprehensible is the mystery! Through the Holy Spirit, our Lord became not God and man but the God-Man. He was truly God manifested in the flesh! That man should be made in God's image was a wonder, but that God should be made in man's image is a greater wonder.

---

15. Handley Carr Glyn Moule, *Outlines of Christian Doctrine* (London: Hodder and Stoughton, 1890), 62.

In his despair, Job cried, *"Neither is there any daysman betwixt us, that might lay his hand upon us both"* (Job 9:33 KJV). But Christ is our Daysman—"The God-Man!" said Dr. Pierson,

> …the daysman betwixt us both, who can lay His hand upon us both, because He is of us both! The way of God to man—the way of man to God; the true Jacob's ladder between heaven and earth, God above it, to come down—man beneath it, to go up! The God-Man is Himself our pledge that as God in Christ became a partaker of the human nature, so man in Christ becomes a partaker of the Divine nature. Born of a woman, made like unto Him! The God-Man is not only a mystery and a miracle but a prophecy and a promise….They used to say of Mozart that he brought angels down; of Beethoven, that he lifted mortals up. Jesus Christ does both, and here lies the central mystery of the God-Man, a mystery which is blessedly revealed to him who by faith has personal experience of His power to save.[16]

And so one side of the mystery of the miracle is that, at the birth of Jesus of Nazareth, there came into existence one personality, such as, with reference to the duality of its nature, had never had existence before, as Dr. Morgan put it.

The Preexistent Christ Born as a Child

The other side of the mystery is that the eternally preexistent Christ was born as a child. We now come to a phase of our holy meditation that fills our hearts with adoring wonder, namely, why and how Christ was begotten apart from the ordinary course of nature. If Christ had come from human parents, such would have meant that He was not existent before His human birth, but that His beginning commenced with His birth. Every child born into the world marks the beginning of a new life, a life that has not existed before. That Christ was the preexistent One is seen clearly in such Scripture passages as John 1:1–3, in which we read, *"He was in the beginning with God"* (verse 2). And so, the virgin birth, because it was not a birth according to natural generation, that is, the result of the sacred relationship of human parents to each other, did not create Christ; it only gave Him who existed from all eternity a human body in which to come and die for all humanity. And as one can easily see, nothing but a virgin birth could produce such a preexistent One.

---

16. Pierson, *"Many Infallible Proofs,"* 264.

Why was it that our Lord condescended to limit Himself in this fashion? Why did He, the preexistent One, take upon Himself the likeness of sinful flesh and commence from the same starting place as ourselves? The answer is that the virgin birth was essential to the redemption and regeneration of humanity. This was described by Dr. Morgan in an excellent way:

> Man's ruin was so terrible and so profound, as witness the darkened intelligence, the deadened emotion, and the degraded will, that there was but one alternative open to the Eternal God. Either He must sweep out and destroy utterly the race or else in infinite patience and through long processes lead it back to Himself. He chose the pathway of reconciliation in His infinite grace, at what cost the story of the Christ alone perfectly reveals....The God-Man then is the gateway between God and man. Through Him, God has found His way back to man, from whom He had been excluded by rebellion. In Him, man finds his way back to God, from whom he had been alienated by the darkening of his intelligence, the death of his love, and the disobedience of his will.[17]

Or we can give the message of our Lord's virgin birth in the following summary, which is enlarged upon in Thomas Watson's *Body of Divinity*, in answer to the question, "Why was Jesus Christ made flesh?"

> The *causa prima*, and impulsive cause, was free grace....Not our deserts but our misery made Christ take flesh....Christ incarnate is nothing but love covered with flesh.
>
> Christ took our flesh upon Him, that He might take our sins upon Him. He was...the greatest sinner, having the weight of the sins of the whole world lying upon Him....
>
> Christ took our flesh that He might make the human nature appear lovely to God, and the divine nature appear lovely to man....
>
> Jesus Christ united Himself to man, that man might be drawn nearer to God.....
>
> He was poor that He might make us rich....He was born of a virgin that we might be born of God. He took our flesh that He might give us

---

17. G. Campbell Morgan, *The Crises of the Christ*, 5th ed. (London: Hodder and Stoughton, 1903), 64–65, 66–67.

the Spirit. He lay in the manger that we might lie in paradise. He came down from heaven that He might bring us to heaven.[18]

And what was all this but love? If our hearts be not rocks, this love of Christ should affect us. Behold love that passes knowledge! Such, then, is the message of our Lord's virgin birth, which we can appreciate only by resting upon the Pillar of Mystery.

18. Thomas Watson, *A Body of Practical Divinity* (Aberdeen: George King, 1838), 179, 181.

2

THE PILLAR OF INCARNATION

"[God] *was manifested in the flesh*...."
—1 Timothy 3:16

The commanding line in the "confession-chant" that Paul quoted in 1 Timothy is made up of only six words in English (only four in Greek), but what a world of tremendous truth is condensed in those few words: "[God] *was manifested in the flesh*"! Is this not a conspicuous illustration of the saying *multum in parvo*—much in small compass? The astounding fact is that when Jesus was manifested in the flesh, He accepted a self-imposed limitation on His own infinite divine powers. He lived on earth in human form, and so fulfilled His Father's will not through the exercise of those powers but through willing obedience directed by the Holy Spirit and a deep knowledge of the Word of God, the Holy Scriptures.

In this way, Jesus set a perfect example for us. We, of course, never had divine powers to begin with. But the distinction does not matter, because Jesus lived a fully obedient human life as if He had never had them, either. The more we understand of this, the more able we will become to rest upon the Pillar of Incarnation and model our lives after His, living in willing obedience to God as directed by the Holy Spirit and the Scriptures.

The way Jesus accepted the limitations of "*being found in human form*" (Philippians 2:8), but still set a perfect example of human obedience, is illustrated most clearly in the account of His temptation in the wilderness. We will therefore devote most of this chapter to a detailed exploration of that experience in His life. But first, once again to dispel the mist, as it were, we will answer some preliminary questions that doubtless arise at the mention of *God* being manifested in the *flesh*. If God was indeed "manifested," then what of God could be seen in Jesus? And how was this different from any way that God had been seen before on the earth?

The book of Genesis tells us that *"God created man in his own image, in the image of God he created him"* (Genesis 1:27). This means that, in some sense, to see a human being was to see something of God. But it does not imply that God has a physical frame such as He fashioned for Adam. While God uses the images of bodily organs, such as eyes, ears, mouth, hands, and feet, in describing His provision and purpose for His children—note, for example, *"The eyes of the LORD are toward the righteous, and his ears toward their cry"* (Psalm 34:15), and *"He who formed the eye, does he not see?"* (Psalm 94:9)—these are intended in only a symbolic sense. Since *"no one has ever seen God"* (John 1:18), we do not know what form, in His person, He possesses. But certainly His divine essence veiled in human form was seen in the various "theophanies" mentioned in the introduction to this book (for example, in Genesis 32:30, when Jacob wrestled with a "man" at Peniel and declared, *"I have seen God face to face, and yet my life is preserved."*).

Before His incarnation, as the only begotten Son of God, Jesus shared the same ethereal form as His Father. But at His birth, God became especially incarnate in His Son—so much so, that Jesus could say, *"He who has seen me has seen the Father"* (John 14:9). This does not mean that God had a human body, such as Jesus took on. The original likeness of God in Adam before the fall, and also that of Jesus to God on earth, represents the possession of the same *spiritual and moral qualities* that God has. *"I and the Father are one"* (John 10:30). All that God is, and was willing to do for man, Jesus came to do. In God we find tender love, melting compassion, and gracious forbearance; we find mercy and power, rectitude and pity, holiness and long-suffering, justice and harmlessness—united. And both the Father and the Son were one in these virtues. This is why, to see God, we should always look at Christ and not anywhere else, not even nature.

Did not Jesus declare to the Father, *"I have manifested thy name"* (John 17:6)? This statement does not infer the mere repetition of a particular name but the nature and being of God—all that God is in Himself. What God is, Jesus manifested to those about Him. This is why He received the name *Immanuel*, which means "God with us." As S. D. Gordon appealingly expressed it:

> [Jesus] was the mind of God thinking out to man. He was the heart of God throbbing love out to man's heart. He was the face of God looking into man's face. He was the voice of God, soft and low, clear and distinct, speaking into man's ears. He was the hand of God, strong and tender, reaching down to take man by the hand....[19]

Or, as Isaac Watts wrote in his hymn "Dearest of All the Names Above":

> Till God in human flesh I see,
> My thoughts no comfort find;
> The holy, just, and sacred Three
> Are terrors to my mind.
>
> But if Immanuel's face appear,
> My hope, my joy begins;
> His name forbids my slavish fear,
> His grace removes my sins.

"WE HAVE BEHELD HIS GLORY"

In one of the most marvelous, yet mysterious, sections of the Bible, we have the record of a man who saw more of God than any other person in history. God said that He knew this privileged man by name. (See Exodus 33:17.) Already, Moses had received assurance from God, who spoke to him *"face to face, as a man speaks to his friend"* (Exodus 33:11), that His divine presence and protection would be with him as he continued to lead Israel to the Promised Land. (See Exodus 33:14–17.) But the deep spiritual nature of Moses craved for something greater, and so he requested, *"I pray thee, show me thy glory"* (Exodus 33:18). All that he had seen of God was insufficient; consequently, he sought for that beatific vision granted as the final reward of those who are perfected in another world.

God, however, could not grant all that Moses desired, for no mortal man could possibly behold the full glory of God and live. He is *"the King...invisible"* (1 Timothy 1:17), *"whom no man has ever seen or can see"* (1 Timothy 6:16). But

---

19. Samuel Dickey Gordon, *Quiet Talks on John's Gospel* (New York: Fleming H. Revell Company, 1915), 51.

God said He would make all His goodness pass before Moses, and He also allowed Moses to witness an actual portion of His glory, as much as anyone could gaze upon, and probably more than any other saint will ever witness until in God's actual presence above. It is to be understood that when God spoke of His face, hands, and back (see Exodus 33:23), the terms were used figuratively in the wonderful climax of the blessed interview between God and His friend. As God's glory passed by, Moses saw the "back" of it, that is, the afterglow of such an effulgence. Ellicott's *Old Testament Commentary* fittingly summarizes the concluding verses of this remarkable episode thus:

> Human nature is, by its very nature, unfit for expression of sublime spiritual truths, and necessarily clothes them in a materialistic garment which is alien to their ethereal nature. All that we can legitimately gather from these verses 22 and 23 is that Moses was directed to a certain retired position, where God miraculously both protected him and shrouded him, while a manifestation of His glory passed by of a transcendent character, and that Moses was allowed to see, not the full manifestation, but the sort of afterglow which is left behind, which was as much as human nature could endure.[20]

Yet the inescapable truth is that in Jesus, His disciples could gaze upon the glory of God and live! *"We have beheld his glory,"* John said, *"glory as of the only Son from the Father"* (John 1:14), the original form of God that Jesus possessed. Paul spoke of Jesus as being *"the image of the invisible God"* (Colossians 1:15) in the same way that, according to John, as the Word, He was the image of the invisible thought of God. Then, in the initial miracle of His public ministry, Jesus turned the water into wine and *"manifested his glory"* (John 2:11). What happened at the wedding feast in Cana of Galilee was the first sign, signally the manifestation of the presence and blessing of the Father in the life of His Son, now shining forth to the eyes and hearts of men. This miracle of love was not performed simply to appeal to the imagination. None of the miracles of Jesus was a mere wonder. Instead, they were visible emblems of all that He was, of all that He came to do as the only begotten Son of the Father. His miracles were radiant images of the permanent miracle of the manifestation of Christ.

---

20. Charles John Ellicott, ed., *An Old Testament Commentary for English Readers* (London: Cassell, Petter, Galpin & Co., 1882), I:316.

To the inner significance of this first public manifestation of His glory, John appended the profound effect upon Jesus' own followers: *"and his disciples believed in him"* (John 2:11). Seeing Him invested with all power and glory as the true Son of the Father, they rested their faith in Him. And so, to quote Godet:

> The glorious irradiations from the person of Jesus, which are called miracles, are, therefore, designed not only, as apologetics often assume, to strike the eyes of the still unbelieving multitude and to stimulate the delaying, but, especially, to illuminate the hearts of believers, by revealing to them, in this world of suffering, all the riches of the living object of their faith.[21]

In another gospel episode, the transfiguration of Jesus, we have the most striking evidence that He came as "God manifested in the flesh." Peter, James, and John were smitten with partial blindness as the brilliant glory of God flashed out in the altered countenance of Jesus and in His garments, which *"became glistening, intensely white, as no fuller on earth could bleach them"* (Mark 9:3). Dazzled, and afraid of such a manifestation of glory, not only in Jesus but in the glorified bodies of Moses and Elijah, the disciples found themselves enveloped by a cloud, and in it they heard God with assuring voice say, *"This is my beloved Son, with whom I am well pleased"* (Matthew 17:5). That trio of privileged disciples saw God's glory reflected in their Master, *and they lived.*

Once they were able to open their half-blinded eyes again, *"they saw no one but Jesus only"* (Matthew 17:8). The glorified heavenly visitants had vanished, as had the flashing out of their Master's inherent glory. Again, He was *Jesus,* with His accustomed form, which they dearly loved. Now, in this age of salvation, no one can truly live without seeing Jesus as the embodiment of both the glory and the grace of God. When Jesus became flesh and dwelt among men, He humanized deity and deified humanity.

Jesus Himself affirmed that *"God is Spirit"* (John 4:24) and that *"a spirit has not flesh and bones"* (Luke 24:39) such as He assumed in His incarnation. When He appeared to His disciples after His resurrection, they were afraid that He was some kind of ghost or phantom, so He invited them to handle Him and to test the reality of His pierced hands and side. How consoled they were when they heard Him say, *"It is I myself"* (Luke 24:39), and saw the evident proofs of

---

21. Frederic Louis Godet, *Commentary on the Gospel of John* (New York: Funk and Wagnalls, 1886), 352.

corporeal resurrection. As they watched Him eat, they realized that Jesus was still in the body He had lived in for over thirty-three years, although now glorified and spiritual—it was manifested under tangible conditions to prove that it was the same body that had been nailed to the cross. (See Luke 24:36–43; John 20:24–28.)

"Flesh and bones" represent the solid and tangible framework of the body. "Blood" is not mentioned, yet the term *"flesh"* implies it. The blood is the life of the animal and corruptible body, which *"cannot inherit the kingdom of God"* (1 Corinthians 15:50). In Luke 24:39, then, *"flesh and bones"* implies the identity, but with diversity of laws, of the resurrection body, which, in some mysterious way, could pass through closed doors. What form God the Father and God the Spirit have eternally possessed is one of the unanswered questions that our entrance into their presence will alone reveal. Meantime, we rest by faith in the statement of Jesus Himself that *"he who has seen me has seen the Father"* (John 14:9).

JESUS ENTERED INTO OUR NATURE

What must be made clear is the fact that as the Word, or *Logos*, Jesus did not lay aside the essence of God—He remained fully divine—but only the form, whatever that is like. He did not pass from the divine state into that of a mere man but entered into our nature, taking upon Himself the likeness of man—not merely assuming such likeness, but *becoming flesh*. Thus, the grand doctrine of John's gospel is that of Jesus as the divine revealer of God entering our humanity, and thereby becoming one with us. The two leading ideas of John in this connection are *testimony* and *faith*, the former for the purpose of the latter. *"They said,… 'Everything that John said about this man was true.' And many believed in him there"* (John 10:41–42). Only the highest could make Himself the lowest, and this is what Jesus accomplished by the union of His eternal divine nature with a human nature. In His incarnation, He became what He was not before—flesh.

The eternal, uncreated Word, who is His divine nature, who was with God in eternity, and who was equal with God, did not join Himself to some human being but became man. Whoever met Him in the days of His flesh met God's Son in human dress. Perfect deity and perfect humanity were His; and, as Godet said:

The content of John's declaration, therefore, is not: two natures or two opposite modes of being co-existing in the same subject; but a single subject passing from one mode to another, in order to recover the first by perfectly realizing the second.[22]

When, at His ascension, He recovered His divine station and state, He did not renounce His human personality but exalted it even to the point where it is the organ of His divine state. Jesus ever remains *"the Man Christ Jesus"* (1 Timothy 2:5).

True faith recognizes in Jesus—the only begotten Son, coming from the presence of His Father—God *revealed* in a human existence. This, without any shadow of doubt, is the foundational truth of the New Testament and is recorded for our inspiration and comfort. On earth, and now in heaven, He is the One ever touched with the feeling of our infirmities, seeing He was tested and tried as we are, and that He added luster to His perfection through suffering. As Henry Twells wrote in the hymn "At Even, When the Sun Did Set":

> O Saviour Christ, Thou too, art man;
> Thou hast been troubled, tempted, tried.
> Thy kind but searching glance can scan
> The very wounds that shame would hide.

"Being found in human form" involved for Jesus being tempted as a human; thus, He was tempted in all points as we have ever been, yet different from us in that He never yielded to any temptation. (See Hebrews 4:15.) In this, He was separate from the sinners He came to save. Although He could confess about His Father, *"I always do what is pleasing to him"* (John 8:29), the testimony of Scripture is that while on earth, as the Son of Man, He *"learned obedience through what he suffered"* (Hebrews 5:8).

Another important fact to remember is that while Jesus remained fully divine when He came to earth, and was active throughout His public ministry in performing miracles through the power of the Holy Spirit for the physical and mental benefit of the afflicted, He limited Himself and never used His divine prerogatives to relieve or satisfy any human need of His own, or to spare Himself from suffering. When we read, *"He himself has suffered and been tempted"* (Hebrews 2:18), the implication is that He drank any bitter cup the Father permitted, to its dregs. *"Shall I not drink the cup which the Father has given me?"* (John 18:11).

---

22. Godet, *Commentary on the Gospel of John*, 270.

A forceful illustration of the self-imposed limitation that Jesus accepted can be found in His temptation, from which, as *"the Man Christ Jesus,"* He emerged victorious. There is no clearer example of resting on the Pillar of Incarnation, of living in willing obedience to God as directed by the Holy Spirit and the Scriptures, than this experience of Jesus. And so we will examine it in detail for the rest of this chapter.

JESUS' EXPERIENCE OF TEMPTATION

To begin with, it is interesting to observe that some of the language Paul used in his epitome of the incarnation in 1 Timothy 3:16 can be found in the temptation record. Christ came as God manifested in the flesh, and twice over He reminded Satan, by quoting the Scriptures, that even though He was visible to the tempter in human form, He was "the Lord his God." When the devil tempted Him to throw Himself off the pinnacle of the temple, Jesus said, *"It is written, 'You shall not tempt the Lord your God,'"* and when the devil tempted Him to worship him, Jesus said, *"It is written, 'You shall worship the Lord your God and him only shall you serve.'"* (See Matthew 4:1–11.) The *"you"* primarily addressed in both of these Scriptures is a loyal servant and worshipper of God, as Jesus was. But, again, the devil was addressed secondarily when Jesus quoted these passages, effectively warning him that he was in the presence of "the Lord his God."

Paul also said that Christ was *"vindicated in the Spirit"* (1 Timothy 3:16), and both Matthew and Luke tell us that Jesus was led by the Spirit into the wilderness to be tempted by the devil. (See Matthew 4:1; Luke 4:1–2.) It was this temptation that vindicated His obedience. Matthew also tells us that when the conflict was over, *"angels came and ministered to him"* (Matthew 4:11). This was one of the many occasions on which Jesus was *"seen by angels"* (1 Timothy 3:16), as we will discuss in detail in chapter 4.

But now, let us look more closely at Satan's threefold attempt to persuade Christ to use His miraculous power as God, not only to prove that He was the "Son of God," but also to alleviate His own physical needs as man—needs He would miraculously supply for other humans in the course of His ministry, as the Gospels go on to record. (See, for example, the feeding of the five thousand, related in each of the Gospels: Matthew 14:13–21; Mark 6:30–44; Luke 9:10–17; John 6:1–14.)

We cannot approach the absorbing experience of Jesus' temptation without being deeply impressed by the marked contrast between the day before Jesus went into the wilderness and the temptations He experienced in the wilderness. On the day of His water baptism by John, there came the simultaneous baptism with the Holy Spirit, with the heavens opening and shedding their radiance upon Him who had come to dwell among us, with the acknowledgment by God that He was His own beloved Son. What a glorious day! But the next day—when He went into the wilderness—what a drastic change, with its hunger, peril, and darkness! Yet it was the heavenly baptism of the first day that prepared Jesus for the hellish battle of the next day. After the dove, there came the devil, but the dove prevailed.

Led by the Spirit into the Wilderness

One cannot consider the unique statement introducing the temptation record—that Jesus was led into the wilderness *by the Holy Spirit* to be tempted—without recalling the quotation from Bishop Hall's *Contemplations*, which Thomas Timpson cited in his remarkable volume on *The Angels of God*—perhaps the most valuable and voluminous study of angelic ministry ever written. The godly bishop exclaimed:

> O the depth of the wisdom of God! How camest Thou, O Savior, to be thus tempted? That Spirit whereby Thou was conceived as Man, and which was one with Thee and the Father as God, led Thee into the wilderness to be tempted of Satan!—And why did it please Thee, O Savior, to fast forty days and forty nights, unless, as Moses fasted forty days at the *delivery* of the Law, and Elijah at the *restitution* of the Law, at the *promulgation* of the gospel, to fulfill the time of both of these types of Thine?[23]

Full of the Holy Spirit, Jesus came to a desert place, so that in its solitude "He might give vent to those sacred passions which the late grand occurrences of the descent of the Spirit upon Him, and the miraculous attestation of a voice from heaven, had such a tendency to inspire," as Doddridge expressed it in his discussion of the temptation account in Luke.[24]

After He had received His inauguration or consecration to office, as well as His Father's attestation at Jordan, the endowment for His three years of public

---

23. Quoted in Thomas Timpson, *The Angels of God: Their Nature, Character, Ranks, and Ministerial Services; as Exhibited in the Holy Scriptures* (London: Aylott and Jones, 1849).
24. Philip Doddridge, *The Family Expositor: Or, A Paraphrase and Version of the New Testament* (London: T. Longman, 1792), 116.

ministry came through the baptism with the Holy Spirit. His Spirit-led temptation should not be approached apart from such baptism, which fortified Him
against His conflict with Satan. Thirty years was a long time to wait for such
a brief period of service, but what momentous events were crowded into such a
short period. Those three years of service among men changed the world.

Only seventeen words, but what contrasts they contain! *"Then Jesus was led
up* [from the Jordan] *by the Spirit into the wilderness to be tempted by the devil"*
(Matthew 4:1). The waters of the Jordan—the arid wilderness! Led by the
Spirit—tempted by the devil! The more one lives under the sway of the Spirit, the
fiercer the assault of Satan. Because no other has ever been so possessed by the
Spirit as Jesus the God-Man was, no other has ever experienced the full anger of
hell as He did. The holier the life, the fiercer the onslaught of the unholy tempter,
who hates, above everything else, victory over his snares and the consequent perfecting of holiness in the hearts of those he tempts.

How arresting is this past participle *"led,"* meaning *guided*! Paul would
have us remember this: *"All who are led by the Spirit of God are sons of God"*
(Romans 8:14). When Jesus became the Son of Man, He revealed Himself as
also the Son of God, when, in unison with the Spirit of God, He went into the
wilderness to be tempted by the devil. Coming as the *"Lamb slain from the foundation of the world"* (Revelation 13:8 KJV), He knew that He would have constant
encounters with the devil until He destroyed his power, so He was not led by the
Spirit against His will; rather, He acquiesced willingly in the Spirit's guidance.

At the beginning of His ministry, Jesus was led by the Spirit to be tempted
by the devil; and at the end of His public career, devil-inspired men led Him out
as a lamb to the slaughter. For ourselves, it is well to yield, at each step of life, to
the divine movings, even when they lead us somewhat mysteriously. The Spirit
still leads us into temptation, for when temptation is not self-invited, and when it
is rightly met, being tempted serves our best interests. It reveals our weaknesses,
rouses our watchfulness, drives us to God for help, clears our aims and principles,
and strengthens the soul in conflict. It is in this way that the machinations of the
devil are overruled for our spiritual good. Isaiah gave us a most appealing symbol
of the Lord's power to use the devil in this way when he told us that the Lord *"will
shave with a razor which is hired"* (Isaiah 7:20). Says Richard Glover: "Temptation
is really, as it were, the string of the kite—something operating as a downward
force, but something without which the kite could not rise."[25]

---

25. Richard Glover, *Lectures on the Lord's Prayer* (London: Religious Tract Society, 1881), 93.

A comparison of the two most prominent temptations in Scripture is most instructive. The first-ever temptation, in Eden, was yielded to, and so began the tragic history of sin in the world, resulting in death and necessitating the second temptation, in the wilderness, which was victoriously resisted and ultimately provided deliverance from sin and death for all who are tempted and defeated by the devil. So both Testaments begin with a record of satanic activity. The first Adam was already full when he was tempted in a beautiful garden, or in a universe yet unspoiled by sin. Hunger was not Adam's susceptibility to temptation, for all the perfect fruits of the garden surrounded him. The *"last Adam"* (1 Corinthians 15:45) was tempted when hungry in a wilderness and yet successfully exhausted all the arts and darts of the wicked one. The temptation of Jesus occurred in "a world rendered desolate by Adam's Fall, and the ultimate effect of His victory will be to make it a garden again."[26] The first temptation is the story of *Paradise lost*; the other of the beginning of *Paradise regained*.

Led; tempted. Leading and testing form a good combination for character building. If we are led by the Spirit, we need have no fear where the foundation is not touched. The oak has no fear of the tempest, if its roots are firm. The first Adam had innocence but fell, because he had a liability toward disobedience against the will and word of God, although not tendency. The last Adam was sinless and thus had neither liability nor tendency. If He could have sinned, then He could not have been our Redeemer. If He could not have been tempted, He could not have been one with us. As for ourselves, we have both liability and tendency to yield to temptation because of inherited and inbred sin, and, therefore, we have more need to watch and pray that we enter not into temptation and be defeated. (See Matthew 26:41; Mark 14:38.) In the words of Horatio Palmer's hymn:

> Yield not to temptation, for yielding is sin;
> Each victory will help you some other to win;
> Fight manfully onward, dark passions subdue,
> Look ever to Jesus, He'll carry you through.

The Enemy's Personality and Power

In Matthew 4, three distinct designations are given our arch-enemy from hell: *"the devil"* (verse 1), *"the tempter"* (verse 3), and *"Satan"* (verse 10). We will

26. John Roberts Dummelow, ed., *A Commentary on the Holy Bible* (New York: Macmillan, 1920), 632.

see, as we now consider each name in detail, how convincingly they prove the personality and power of the persistent adversary of Jesus, who, though unseen, is yet real and ever full of malignity, even when he appears as an *"angel of light"* (2 Corinthians 11:14). The devil in the traditional representation is a creature with a horned head, cloven-hoofed feet, and a tail. But if that were his real appearance, he would be too hideous and obvious to deceive anyone. The devil of the Bible is repulsive morally, but he may be attractive physically. This dangerous being is apparently one of the cherubim that God created to serve Himself, a being anointed for a position of great authority, possibly over the primitive creation, but who fell through pride and ambition and was expelled from heaven (see Isaiah 14:12–15; Ezekiel 28:11–19) and who, ever since, has been the tireless enemy of both God and man.

The word *"devil"* is from the Greek *diabolos*, meaning "accuser" or "slanderer," from a root meaning "to throw over" or "to cast down"; and, true to this foul name, he tempted Jesus to cast Himself down from the pinnacle of the temple. The name is also related to his own rebellion and rejection, seeing that he was cast out of heaven and then made the earth and the air the scene and seat of his unceasing diabolical activity. (See, for example, Luke 10:18; Ephesians 2:2; 1 Peter 5:8.)

As for Jesus, the devil could not throw Him down; and now, blessedly secure in the heavens, He is able to lift up the needy out of the devil's dunghill. (See Psalm 113:7; 147:6.) At Calvary, the tempter was still the *diabolos*, the one who casts down, for the taunt of the unbelievers he held captive was, *"Let him come down now from the cross, and we will believe in him"* (Matthew 27:42). But Jesus willingly stayed on His cross of shame and suffering for our sins, and it is only faith in what He did for us that avails. *"I, when I am lifted up from the earth, will draw all men to myself"* (John 12:32).

Such a dreaded name as *"tempter"* can validly be applied to humans as well as to the devil and demons, but Matthew names the heartless foe of God and men as *the* tempter, seeing that he is the chief malignant enticer who untiringly labors for the destruction of men. He is weak in that he can harm us only by making us harm ourselves, but strong in his power of persuading us to do so—a persuasion that had no influence whatsoever over the tempted Christ. Subtle, as is a tempter, he chose a fitting time for his assault, namely, immediately after Christ's baptism, indicating for us that consecration to God incites such temptation as all the arts of hell can produce to slay a person's dedication to God.

The tempter also knew that Jesus, in His hungry condition after such a long fast, would be weak and physically least fit to resist the temptation to appease His hunger miraculously. As God, Christ could not be tempted with evil. (See James 1:13.) Therefore, in order to be *"in every respect...tempted as we are"* (Hebrews 4:15), He met the tempter in His human nature, weak though he was, and conquered him by the enabling power of the Spirit. This is the clearest possible example of the Pillar of Incarnation, on which Jesus rested when He lived in human flesh obediently to God through the empowerment of the Spirit.

We might well wonder what it was that animated and emboldened the tempter to assail Christ as he did. Perhaps he thought he would obtain as easy a victory over this last Adam as he had over the first Adam in Paradise. Further, with the remembrance of his own fall, he might have arrogantly concluded that no heart, even one that was "meek and lowly," could resist the temptations of pride and ambition. But how deluded the tempter was! Doddridge wrote,

> Could he, who afterwards proclaimed Christ to be the Son of the Most High God, and had perhaps but lately heard Him owned as such by a voice from heaven, make any doubt of His Divinity? Or if he actually believed it, could he expect to vanquish Him? We may rather conclude that he did not expect it; but mad with rage and despair, he was determined at least to worry that Lamb of God, which he knew he could not devour; and to vex, with his hellish suggestions, that innocent and holy soul, which he knew he could never seduce.[27]

Many sincere Christians have been somewhat perplexed over the seeming contradiction between the Holy Spirit leading Jesus into temptation and the petition Jesus taught His disciples to ask of God, *"Lead us not into temptation"* (Matthew 6:13). This cannot mean freedom from conflict with the tempter; otherwise, the statement that Jesus was *"tempted as we are"* (Hebrews 4:15) would not be true. Ellicott's *Commentary*, at Matthew 6:13, seems to have a satisfactory answer to this apparent problem. It points out that the Greek word for *"temptation"* includes two different thoughts that are represented by the same word *trial* in English. The first thought is of allurements, based on human pleasures, that tend to lead us into evil. James teaches us not to think of temptation in which lust meets opportunity as anything that God would ever lead us into. (See James 1:13–14.) That is why it is so shocking to think of asking Him not

27. Doddridge, *Family Expositor*, 124–125.

to lead us into temptation of this kind. But there is another thought behind the Greek word for temptation or trial: sufferings that test or try us, up to or perhaps beyond the limits of our strength (for example, Matthew 26:41: *"Watch and pray that you may not enter into temptation; the spirit indeed is willing, but the flesh is weak."*). This is the more common meaning of the term in the New Testament, and it is what we must think of here.

Persecution, spiritual conflicts, agony of body or of spirit—these may come to us as a test or as a discipline. Should we shrink from them? An ideal stoicism, a perfect faith, would say, "No, let us accept these and leave the issue in our Father's hands." But those who are conscious of their weaknesses cannot shake off the fear that they might fail in the conflict, and the cry of that conscious weakness is therefore, "Lead us not into such trials," even as our Lord prayed, *"My Father, if it be possible, let this cup pass from me"* before adding, *"Nevertheless, not as I will, but as thou wilt"* (Matthew 26:39).

The answer to the prayer may come either directly in actual exemption from the trial or in *"the way of escape"* (1 Corinthians 10:13), or the strength to bear it. It is hardly possible to read the Lord's Prayer without thinking of the experience of temptation through which our Lord had just passed. The memory of that trial in all its terrible aspects was still present with Him, and in His tender love for His disciples, He bade them pray that they may not be led into anything so awful. (The paired phrases, *"Lead us not into temptation, but deliver us from evil,"* or *"the evil one"* [NKJV], can be understood to mean that we seek deliverance from the sinister evil lurking in any approach of the tempter.) But what must be made clear is the fact that as a human being, and particularly through His own experience of temptation, Christ acquired the experiential ability to *"help those who are tempted"* (Hebrews 2:18).

With the third temptation, the resistance of Jesus was roused to the utmost pitch of holy indignation, and He ordered, *"Begone, Satan!"* (Matthew 4:10). By uttering this most dreaded, yet revealing, name, "plucking the mask from the foe, who had assumed his fairest form to do his foulest deed, Jesus flung it away, and left the naked wretch a convicted fiend."[28] Up to now, "He had borne the devil's insults and temptations with singular patience; He had replied to him with mildness and gentleness," said Timpson in his work on *The Angels of God*, "but now the blasphemous audacity could no longer be endured: the holiness of

---

28. James Bennett, *Lectures on the History of Jesus Christ*, 2nd ed. (London: Westley and Davis, 1828), 1:101.

the Redeemer obliged Him to show His resentment, and exert His power to rid Himself of so vile a creature," and so He commanded, *"Begone, Satan!"*

In his epic poem *Paradise Lost*, Milton described how this once choicest of all the glorious seraphs was "brighter once amidst the host/of Angels, than that star the stars among" (7:132–133). But the poet also spoke of his fall:

> Satan, so call him now; his former name
> Is heard no more in heaven: he of the first,
> If not the first archangel; great in power
> In favor and pre-eminence.
>
> (5:658–661)

This created but superhuman angelic being is represented in Scripture as the avowed adversary of the Triune God of Scripture, of the saints, and of all ennobling virtues. The name *Satan* means "adversary," and the apostles thought of him in that way. Peter, in particular, centered on Satan's ferocity as an enemy when he warned us, *"Be sober, be watchful. Your adversary the devil prowls around like a roaring lion, seeking some one to devour"* (1 Peter 5:8). Mark, in his description of the temptation, said that Jesus was *"with the wild beasts"* (Mark 1:13). Those wild beasts perhaps were made more ferocious at that time by the *"roaring lion"* who himself could not harm Jesus, the cocreator of the beasts of the field. The wild beasts knew that Jesus could calm them as He did for Daniel. By His victory over these wild beasts and the roaring lion, He regained for humanity the empire over the beasts that the first Adam lost. *"The wolf shall dwell with the lamb, and the leopard shall lie down with the kid….They shall not hurt or destroy in all my holy mountain"* (Isaiah 11:6, 9).

As Satan, then, such an adversary stands in his true character; and Jesus "no longer deals with him as a pretended friend and pious counselor, but calls him by his right name—His knowledge of which from the outset He had carefully concealed till now—and orders him off."[29] The truth Satan heard then, that allegiance is due to God and to Him only, Peter had to learn when he sought to turn his Master from the appointed path of suffering. Unconsciously, the apostle became the mouthpiece of Satan and had the sorrow of hearing himself rebuked with the selfsame words of the third temptation: *"Get behind me, Satan!"*

---

29. Robert Jamieson, Andrew Robert Fausset, and David Brown, *A Commentary: Critical, Practical and Explanatory, on the Old and New Testaments: New Testament*, vol. 1 (Toledo: Jerome B. Names, 1883), 263.

(Matthew 16:23). But the utterance of such a command for the first time in the wilderness implies that in all previous temptations the wicked one had presented himself in disguise, but there he was revealed as Satan in all his nakedness and absolute antagonism to the divine will.

Returning to the three temptations of the Incarnate One by Satan, their nature can be compared to John's description of the three classes of sins in the world, found in 1 John 2:16:

The first temptation: *"the lust of the flesh."* (See Matthew 4:1–4.)

The second temptation: *"the lust of the eyes."* (See Matthew 4:5–7.)

The third temptation: *"the pride of life."* (See Matthew 4:8–11.)

These three direct attacks of Satan, the adversary, require our close and reverent attention, seeing that they were designed to induce Jesus to act from Himself, totally independent of His Father and of the Holy Spirit, and so not to rest on the Pillar of Incarnation. The first two temptations specifically were efforts by the devil to force Jesus to call upon miraculous powers in order to prove that He was the Son of God. Sinless though He was, His human hunger made Him susceptible to feel the first temptation; because He had such strong faith, He felt the second; and because of His great love and pity for mankind, He felt the third. Let us now consider each of the temptations reverently and in detail.

THE FIRST TEMPTATION: DISTRUST

This temptation was to distrust. It was personal, and it was associated with the body, or the natural, physical life of Jesus. The notation that *"he fasted forty days and forty nights, and afterward he was hungry"* (Matthew 4:2) explains the aim of the devil's first assault. "Fasting" can mean a spare diet, such as John the Baptist practiced, for Jesus said of him that he came *"neither eating nor drinking"* (Matthew 11:18), yet John had his *"locusts and wild honey"* (Matthew 3:4). But "fasting" can also imply total abstinence from food, which is likely what Jesus' fast for forty days and forty nights entailed. While absorbed with the contemplation of the great task He was now facing, Jesus did not find the need for food. (The same thing happened to a lesser extent during His ministry; see Mark 3:20–21 and John 4:31–32.) But when those days were over, and the strain of thought and prayer ceased, Jesus found Himself helpless and feeble through lack of bodily sustenance. It was then, when He was physically least able to resist, that the strong enemy came.

It is clearly seen that the tempter adapted his strategy to the circumstances of the hour, namely, when Jesus was keenly feeling the craving of hunger. Jesus had unlimited power to work miracles under the direction of the Father and through the empowerment of the Spirit, as is seen in the Scriptures later on when He took a few small loaves and fishes and fed thousands of very hungry people who had gathered to hear Him. So, why not make bread for Himself? In effect, the devil said, "If it is right to feed others who are hungry, why is it wrong to feed Yourself? If You are a miracle-worker, command these stones to become bread to meet Your need of food." Such reasoning implied, "If You do not take this matter into Your own hands, You're a dead man."

Perhaps we do not realize sufficiently that the worst temptations are those associated with seemingly harmless actions. As Richard Glover pointed out, one of the greatest lessons we need to learn in this life is that every act that is done from wrong motives is wrong, however innocent in itself it may seem to be. Thus, in this first temptation, the only wrong in the act would be the feelings prompting it.

The devil called upon Jesus to *command* the stones at His feet to be made bread. Yet no command would have been necessary, for He would have easily made those stones into loaves, as He changed water into wine without any word or visible action on His part. He just willed the transformation to take place. In the words of Richard Crashaw's poem,

> When Christ at Cana's feast, by power divine
> Inspired cold water with the warmth of wine,
> See! cried they, while in reddening tide it gushed,
> The bashful stream hath seen its God and blushed.

Again, such a silent change would have been the same with the stones becoming bread; but, had Jesus yielded to the satanic suggestion, He would have taken Himself out of God's hands and made Himself unlike His brethren, whose bodily nature He had taken. Humans need a Savior to stand with them in their need and to teach them how to endure temptation and how to trust. Jesus would not have been such a Savior had He yielded to the devil. And so, in the words of Richard Chenevix Trench's aptly named poem "Christ's Restraint,"

> Time was, and He who nourished crowds with bread
> Would not one meal unto Himself afford.

We have already indicated that Jesus never performed a miracle for self-advantage or used spiritual power to supply His own material needs. Had He done so, He would have forsaken that reliance upon God that was the primary condition of His assumption of our humanity, His incarnation. The simple doing for His own comfort what the poor and needy could not do would have cut the link that unites Him to us. So that act, in itself harmless, would, in these circumstances, have severed Him at once from God and from man. It was alone for the good of others that miraculous power was entrusted to Jesus, and the Gospels confirm His strict economy of such power. This first temptation, then, was designed to force Him to forsake the humanity in which He had come to live, die, and rise again—and He rejected that temptation, in order to fulfill the purpose of His incarnation.

It will be further observed that the first two temptations began with the same formula, namely, *"If you are the Son of God..."* (Matthew 4:3, 6). The word *"if"* suggests doubt, but the tempter had no doubt whatsoever as to the true identity of Jesus as the only begotten of the Father. Just before the wilderness conflict, the Father bore witness not only to Christ's messiahship but also to His eternal, divine sonship: *"This is my beloved Son, with whom I am well pleased"* (Matthew 3:17). But the devil seemed to challenge this adulation by urging Jesus to prove the reality of such a blessed sonship. Making bread out of stones and leaping from the pinnacle of the temple were to be crucial tests of this sonship—efforts to dislodge from His heart the consciousness of His relation to the Father. But the devil did not require the exhibition of these acts as evidence of Christ's sonship, for from the dateless past, he knew Him to be equal with God.

That the same is equally true of all evil spirits, or fallen angels, is clear from the cure of the demoniac described in Mark 1:21–28. In the synagogue at Capernaum in which Jesus had been authoritatively teaching truths that caused the worshippers to be astonished, there was among them a man with an impure spirit or demon. (Alas! This was not the first time, or the last, that an evil spirit possessed a pew-holder.) The character of impurity is ascribed to evil spirits some twenty times in the Gospels. As Jesus came to expel this particular spirit from the man possessed, the spirit cried out, *"What have you to do with us, Jesus of Nazareth? Have you come to destroy us? I know who you are, the Holy One of God"* (Mark 1:24).

No wonder this agent of the devil asked, *"What have you to do with us?"* Jesus had nothing in common with hell. The question implied the entire separation of interests and values between the Holy One of God and unclean spirits. The reaction of the demon to its expulsion from the man presents a striking feature of the miracle, namely, that of the testimony of the powers of darkness to the deity and humanity of our Lord:

"Jesus of Nazareth." This was the way the crowds commonly referred to Jesus. (See, for example, Luke 18:37.) Looking upon His human form, everyone could see that the unclean spirit used this title correctly in describing Him as a Man born in Nazareth. But then, in a remarkable way, there follows hell's confirmation of the messiahship of Jesus and its strictest meaning!

"The Holy One of God." The demon knew that Jesus was the Holy One of God and acknowledged Him as such, the One who had attained the highest form of holiness and divinity. He was, indeed, the God-Man.

The rebuke and command of Jesus aroused the rage of this unclean spirit, who knew only too well that the Holy One he faced was unafraid of the devil and all his apostate angels. Jesus ordered him, *"Be silent!"* (Mark 1:25). This term literally means "be muzzled or gagged." (The same verb is used for the calming of the winds and the waves in Mark 4:39.) What a display of deity this expulsion was! The people were amazed at Jesus' authority and power, and quickly the news spread abroad that evil spirits were forced to obey Him. By His incarnation, which He lived out so effectively in response to this first temptation, Jesus sealed the doom of the devil and his evil hosts. *"The ruler of this world is judged"* (John 16:11).

As for the devil himself, although he is *"a liar and the father of lies"* (John 8:44), instead of saying, *"If you are the Son of God,"* he could have truthfully confessed, "I know You are the Holy One of God," for, again, he knew Him only too well. At the creation of the angelic host by the Trinity, it is clearly evident that the devil, a created being, was not created a devil but as one endowed with position, dignity, and honor. The phrases used of him in his originally created state, such as *"day star, son of the morning"* (Isaiah 14:12 RV), *"the anointed cherub"* (Ezekiel 28:14 RV, KJV, NKJV), and *"perfect in beauty"* (Ezekiel 28:12), can apply only to the highest of all angelic beings.

Does it not seem as if the dominion of this world, as it was originally created, was given to the devil while he was yet a holy angel named Lucifer, meaning "Light Bearer"—a position Jesus Himself recognized when He called him *"the ruler of this world"* (John 12:31; 14:30; 16:11)? But the catastrophe overtaking

God's original creation, as described in Genesis 1 and 2, came as the result of the devil's rebellion in heaven. From Isaiah 45:18, which says that God "*formed the earth and made it (he established it; he did not create a chaos),*" it is apparent that the earth was not originally "*without form and void*" (Genesis 1:2), but that it became so as the result of a terrible upheaval. The remainder of the first chapter in the Bible is the record of the production of *cosmos* out of *chaos*, to fit it for its new inhabitants and rulers. (See Genesis 1:26–28.) The Apocrypha aptly says that "through the devil's envy death entered the world" (Wisdom of Solomon 2:24), for the devil's only chance of retaining dominion lay in making man a rebel like himself, which he did when the first Adam disobeyed a divine command.

But in a past eternity, when all was perfect bliss and harmony, the devil, when he was still the angel Lucifer, praised and honored the three Persons of the blessed Trinity. "*Praise him, all his angels*" (Psalm 148:2). Receiving their praises was the only begotten of the Father, as well as the Father Himself, and the "*son of the morning*" joined in those praises to the eternal Son of God. Thus the devil knew all about the wonderful love and union that had existed between the Father and the Son, and so he knew Jesus to be God's well-beloved Son only too well. And the devil could see that even on earth, Jesus, being heaven-born, of whom the Father said, "*I have begotten thee*" (Hebrews 1:5), had the full effulgence of glory surrounding Him.

When God proclaimed His Son to be His Vice-Regent, with Himself as Supreme Ruler in heaven and on earth, and with Lucifer the high angel as under-ruler over creation, can it be that Lucifer had expected to be given the post of honor that was assigned to God the Son and to become next in honor, majesty, and power to God the Supreme, so that it was at this time that his jealous hatred for the Son was born? The murderous hatred toward Jesus that burned in the hearts of the Pharisees was born of the arch-hater of Jesus, namely, the devil. Without fear, Jesus told those who sought to kill Him that they were children of the devil. (See John 8:44.) However, what is so instructive about Jesus during His contact with the devil during His temptation is the comfort He found for His own heart in Scripture and likewise the answers the Bible provided for the satanic suggestions presented.

Is there not the air of irrevocability, or finality, about this three-word declaration, "*It is written,*" spoken to the devil three times by Jesus? (See Matthew 4:4, 7, 10.) Scripture is irreversible. Pilate's irrevocable dictum is far truer of the revelation of God: *"What I have written I have written!"* (John 19:22). Scripture is God's complete, final, and unalterable Word to the world, with its original copy in heaven. God's Word is indestructible. Humans may try to destroy it, as King Jehoiakim sought to do by cutting into pieces and burning the scroll that bore Jeremiah's words (see Jeremiah 36:23), but they can never succeed, because the written Word, like the Living Word Himself, lives and abides forever. (See 1 Peter 1:23 NKJV.)

In His response to the overtures of the devil, Jesus has left us an example that we should *"follow in his steps"* (1 Peter 2:21), namely, that if we, too, would be victorious over the wiles of the devil, we must know how to use *"the sword of the Spirit, which is the word of God"* (Ephesians 6:17). Jesus did not enter into the pros and cons of each proposal of the devil; in each case, He just quoted a passage of Scripture, and the tempter was silenced. Jesus lived in the will of God, as revealed in the Word of God, and thus defeated the enemy. Because Jesus was saturated in Scripture, He was, as W. H. Griffith Thomas expressed it, able to discern the principles at stake in the given situation; the speciousness of temptation, whether of self or of Satan; and the shallowness of life that would result from yielding. In union with the Scripture-loving Lord, we, too, can be more than conquerors over the world, the flesh, and the devil.

Our Lord's first apt choice of a Scripture to meet the subtle suggestion of the devil reveals His identity with the humanity of which He had become a part for its salvation from sin. As Man, He felt the pangs of hunger but still said, *"Man shall not live by bread alone, but by every word that proceeds from the mouth of God"* (Matthew 4:4; see also Deuteronomy 8:3). Even the Son of Man Himself needed material substance for the body, but spiritual food was for Him a prime and prior necessity. With Job, of old, He could confess, *"I have not departed from the commandment of his lips; I have treasured in my bosom the words of his mouth"* (Job 23:12). Because of the constitution of the body, material food is necessary for existence; but man also has a soul requiring spiritual sustenance, and because the soul has precedence over the body, in the spiritual realm, food for the soul has the preeminence. Thus, the experience of Jesus in the wilderness clothed the history of the manna, the *"bread from heaven"* (Exodus 16:4), that God sent for Israel, with a new significance. *"Every word that proceeds from the mouth of God"* implies that Scripture, as a whole, is the miracle-working Word of God. The first Adam had every tree of the garden for food, but he still fell; the last Adam had only desert stones to mock His hunger, yet He conquered His foe.

The blessed truth, then, emerging from this first temptation is that, as the Son of God with power, Jesus could have made bread out of stones to satisfy His hunger and sustain His physical life and, by the exercise of such a power, revealed that He was the conscious possessor of miraculous gifts. But, had He yielded to the request of the devil, He would have been guilty of self-assertion and distrust, as well as the denial of the sonship recently affirmed at His baptism. (See Matthew 3:16–17.) As to His initial use of Scripture against the devil, no Old Testament passage could have been so appropriate to His purpose than the one He chose from Deuteronomy. It was as if He argued with His own heart in this way, as suggested by Jamieson's *Commentary*:

> Now, if Israel spent, not forty days, but forty years in a waste, howling wilderness, where there were no means of human subsistence, not starving, but divinely provided for, on purpose to prove to every age that human support depends not upon bread, but upon God's unfailing Word of promise and pledge of all needful providential care, am I, distrusting this Word of God, and despairing of relief, to take the law into my own hand? True, the Son of God is able enough to turn stones into bread: but what the Son of God is able to do is not the present question, but what is *man's duty* under want of the necessaries of life. And as Israel's condition in the wilderness did not justify their unbelieving murmurings and frequent desperation, so neither would mine warrant the exercise of the power of God in snatching despairingly at unwarranted relief. As man, therefore, I will await Divine supply, nothing doubting that at the fitting time it will arrive.[30]

THE SECOND TEMPTATION: PRESUMPTION

Though Jesus was the Sinless One, His extreme hunger caused Him to feel the first temptation; but it was because of His obedience to God and His Word that He deeply felt this second assault of the enemy, which had a national character. Because Jesus was victorious by faith when He was assailed through His bodily sufferings, the devil next endeavored to make such faith overdo itself in presumption, and so he appealed to Jesus' spiritual exaltation.

Just how the tempter took Jesus up to the high place of the temple in the Holy City—the metropolis of all Jewish worship—we are not told. Whatever shape of

---

30. Jamieson, *Commentary*, 23.

personality or substance the devil possessed is beyond our present knowledge. The consistent truth of Scripture is that he is a personal devil and can assume borrowed shapes and subtle transformation to achieve his evil purposes, just as he used Peter to try to dissuade his Master from going to the cross. Are we not warned never to be ignorant of his clever devices? (See 1 Corinthians 2:11 KJV.)

This further temptation starts from the attestation of the character of Jesus as the Son of God—a sonship He constantly affirmed and was always determined not to be disputed out of, even by the son of perdition, who knew only too well the eternal relationship between the Father and the Son. Had Jesus succumbed to the wiles of the devil, then He would have become a prodigal Son and unworthy of becoming the Savior of the world.

Early church literature records a curious coincidence: that James the Just, the brother of Jesus, was thrown down from a high platform of the temple into one of the courts below and was crushed to death (Eusebius, *Ecclesiastical History* 2:23). It would have been the same fate for Jesus, without any miraculous intervention. The lofty position overlooking the temple courts was a most convenient point from which a multitude could be addressed, so the devil suggested to Jesus that He should preach to the gathered multitudes below from this great height, then prove His messianic claims beyond all question by flying through the air and reaching the ground unharmed. But, had Jesus leapt from the lofty pulpit as a man, He would have been killed after hitting the stone pavement, unless He had called upon miraculous forces to ensure a safe, unharmed landing. This shortcut to acceptance by the people would be welcomed by them and was commended to Jesus by the devil as being quite safe, easy, and effective, with a Scripture promise guaranteeing a delightful flight and a victorious landing. Thus, as Dummelow's *Commentary* summarized this satanic approach:

> Stripped of its symbolical form, this was a temptation to take a short and easy road to recognition as the Messiah by giving "a sign from heaven" which even the most incredulous and unspiritual would be compelled to accept. This short and easy method Jesus decisively rejected. He determined to appeal to the spiritual apprehension of mankind, that they might believe on Him, not because they were astounded by His miracles and could not resist their evidence, but because they were attracted by the holiness and graciousness of His character, by the loftiness of His teaching, and by the love of God to man which was manifested in all His

words and actions. He intended His miracles to be secondary, an aid to the faith of those who on other grounds were inclined to believe, but not portents to extort the adhesion of those who had no sympathy with Himself or His aims.[31]

For us, the lesson at this point is obvious. The same temptation comes to us when a sinister voice urges us to take liberties with God or to parade our virtues or to pursue any course that is morally perilous, with the idea that God will intervene and keep us from being destroyed. Many who do not fall through despair fall through presumption, because their pride renders the temptation more seductive.

But is there not a further interpretation of this second temptation for us to consider? Satan tried to persuade Jesus to throw Himself down because he could not push Him down; was this not another effort to kill Him before the death of the cross that Jesus was willing to suffer, but which the devil did not want, seeing that by Jesus' death and resurrection his own fate would be sealed? That the devil bore intense hatred for God's beloved Son from the beginning of his evil career forms a great and important subject of Bible study, as we will now see briefly.

From the first proclamation of the redemption evangel, declaring that the seed of the woman would bruise the serpent's head (see Genesis 3:15), Satan, symbolized as the serpent, set about the destruction of the royal seed from which Jesus was to come, and he almost succeeded. Many devices and arts were conceived in order to exterminate the seed that would ultimately produce Satan's great Antagonist and Glorious Conqueror. If ever the devil and his angels had a bad day, it was on the day that Jesus was "born of a woman"—the realization of the promise that her seed would destroy the authority and power of the devil. Here was a marvel: a Child divinely conceived and born, and all at once the devil's murderous energies are aroused, and his subtle wisdom used for the attempt to slaughter Mary's renowned Infant under Herod's edict to kill all helpless babies. (See Matthew 2:16.)

As we know, the holy Babe was divinely spared. Yet the enemy was bent on further murderous attacks, and this present temptation appears to have been one of them. By His sudden appearance in the temple courts, Jesus would obtain power and popularity; and as to any possibility of destroying Himself in descending, had not God promised angelic guardianship? But this device to identify Jesus

---

31. Dummelow, *Commentary on the Holy Bible*, 633.

with vainglory, spectacular fame, and distrust was thwarted by the *"one stronger than he"* (Luke 11:22).

Later on, the startling word was brought to Jesus: *"Herod wants to kill you"* (Luke 13:31). Yet poor Herod was but the devil's tool; and his fox-like character, reflected in the knavish craftiness of the Pharisees, was a gift of the devil. But the death edict of Herod met this challenge by Jesus: *"Go and tell that fox,...'I must go on my way today and tomorrow and the day following'"* (Luke 13:32–33). In effect, He was saying, "Tell the devil and his demons that I am immortal until My work is done." Then we have statements that tell of additional attempts on Jesus' life, such as: *"[They] took counsel together in order to arrest Jesus by stealth and kill him"* (Matthew 26:4). *"The Pharisees went out, and immediately held counsel with the Herodians against him, how to destroy him"* (Mark 3:6). *"And they...led him to the brow of the hill on which their city was built, that they might throw him down head-long"* (Luke 4:29). *"They took up stones to throw at him"* (John 8:59).

Jesus had to die; but it was a death ordained by God, *"that through death he might destroy him who has the power of death, that is, the devil"* (Hebrews 2:14)—in other words, it was a death by which He was to destroy death forever. All of the devil's premature efforts to kill Jesus before the cross failed simply because it had been decreed that He should die on the cross. It is thus that this death at Calvary differs from all other deaths. Others *suffer* death; Jesus *achieved* it. Death comes to cut short the life of humans and frustrate their aims and ambitions; but Jesus, by His death, consummated, crowned, and completed His work. Hence His triumphant cry as He expired: *"It is finished!"* (John 19:30 NKJV).

The devil's last great attempt to destroy God's magnificent and perfect plan of redemption was to make sure that Jesus remained dead. So the sepulcher was made secure, the stone sealed, and guards set to watch it. But this effort to keep that sacred and scarred body sealed in a tomb was defeated, for, in the words of Robert Lowry's hymn "Low in the Grave He Lay," "Death could not keep its prey," and so, on the third day, "He arose a victor from the dark domain." How our devil-beset hearts are continuously comforted by Jesus' words, *"I am the first and the last, and the living one; I died, and behold I am alive for evermore, and I have the keys of Death and Hades"* (Revelation 1:17–18).

Satanic subtlety in this second temptation is found in the tempter's use of Scripture. Was there not a seeming scriptural warrant for the dramatic, crucial test of sonship in the declaration of the psalmist that angelic hosts would bear up, or surround, or protect God's Chosen One from danger or death? (See Psalm 91:11–12.) Satan's quotation, as far as it went, was in harmony with the Hebrew original; but what he cunningly omitted from the promise was the phrase *"to guard you in all your ways,"* for he knew only too well that if Jesus had succumbed to his appeal, it would not have been one of *His* ways.

Bishop Joseph Hall, reading of the devil's use of Scripture, exclaimed, "But what is this I see? Satan himself with a Bible in under his arm and a text in his mouth!"[32] When Satan is seen thus, he is up to no good purpose, for he is expert at using, or misusing, Scripture to his own advantage—a "good theologian." He approached Jesus craftily and is the father of all who *"tamper with God's word"* (2 Corinthians 4:2). How able he is to pervert and obscure the true significance of Scripture, to sow *"weeds among the wheat"* (Matthew 13:25). It is apparent that, stung by his defeat through the power of the Word of God in his first endeavor to tempt Jesus, the devil was eager to try the effect of Scripture from his own mouth.

However, Satan's thrust of the sword of the Spirit was made ineffective by the way Jesus handled the same weapon of spiritual warfare: *"**Again** it is written"* (Matthew 4:7). He did not reply by filling in for the devil the unquoted part of the portion he used. Jesus knew that he had omitted *"to guard you in all your ways."* With great calm, however, He broke the force of this satanic onslaught by quoting another Scripture, for the entire Word of God was known to Him.

From the answer of Jesus, it is evident that the devil's design was to urge Him to prove that He was the Son of God by forcing His Father to send angels for His preservation. As we have already suggested, the devil sought to destroy Jesus and would have gladly hurled Him from the parapet to a frightful death below, but he dared not to make the attempt, for he knew that the One before him was *"stronger than he."* Therefore, he tried to encourage Jesus in a spirit of presumption, but Jesus perceived his evil intent and replied simply for His rebuke, *"You shall not tempt the Lord your God"* (Matthew 4:7).

Jesus promised His disciples that when the Holy Spirit came as His ascension gift, one aspect of the Spirit's ministry would be to bring to the remembrance of the believer the truths of Holy Scripture. But He had no need of this specific office of the Spirit Himself, for in Him the written Word and the Living Word were one. The simple word *"again"* implies that Jesus meant this in His

---

32. Quoted in Jamieson, *Commentary*, 24.

reply to the devil: "The Scripture you have quoted is true, and on its promise I implicitly rely; but in using it, there is another Scripture that you must not forget." This particular Scripture that Jesus quoted has a special historical reference: "*You shall not put the LORD your God to the test, as you tested him at Massah*" (Deuteronomy 6:16).

The specific sin of the people at Massah was their unwillingness to believe that the presence of God was real until they saw supernatural evidence of it. Thus, the question they asked, "*Is the LORD among us or not?*" (Exodus 17:7), sprang from their unbelief. In using the Scripture from Deuteronomy 6, then, Jesus implied, as He related it to Himself, that to demand a proof of God's care in the way the devil suggested would have identified Him with a spirit of distrust like the people had manifested at Massah. One lesson Jesus learned as a human was to commit Himself absolutely to His Father's will. This commitment led Him later to refuse the aid of twelve legions of angels, which the Father would have gladly sent for His Son's protection. (See Matthew 26:53.) Jamieson's *Commentary* observes:

> Preservation in danger is divinely pledged: shall I then *create* danger, either to put the promised security skeptically to the proof, or wantonly to demand a display of it? That were "to tempt the Lord my God," which, being expressly forbidden, would forfeit the right to expect preservation.[33]

There is an aspect of this second temptation, however, that seems to lay hold of my mind with an irresistible force, namely, that it provides a further evidence of Jesus as "God manifested in flesh." In respect to His *humanity*, He was still suffering from the pang of the physical suffering (hunger) that He had refused to relieve in a miraculous way. As a Man, He was being tempted in all points as ordinary men are, but never yielding to temptation as even the best of men do. As for an expression of His *deity*, He ever was the Son of God. Yet in the passage He quoted to the devil who was tempting Him, as we saw earlier, He spoke words that could be applied to Himself when He said, "*You shall not tempt the Lord your God*"—in other words, "You shall not tempt Me, I who am the Lord your God." Think of it: "your God"! Yes, Jesus was God even to the devil, who, although he was a roaring lion prowling around to devour, was but a lion on a leash and could not go beyond divine permission, as evidenced by the command Jesus used in the next temptation: "*Begone, Satan!*" (Matthew 4:10). That was the fiat of the God-Man.

---

33. Jamieson, *Commentary*, 262.

The central lesson for our own hearts is obvious. We are forbidden to experiment with God. As Dr. Richard Glover expressed it in his commentary on Matthew, "Jesus will take no liberties with God." He will expect angels to protect Him in "every way on which God sends Him," but He would not ask them, dare not expect them, to protect Him if He were to run needless risks from motives of spiritual pride. Too often, we take liberties: sinning willfully, in the hope that, after all, grace will not be withdrawn; or going into temptation and risking safety of soul, in the hope that some angel will prevent our coming to harm. Learn the Savior's way: "No liberties with God," no self-display. The lowly path of duty is to be preferred to the ostentatious path of seeming faith. Remember the solemn words of Moses: "*The person who does anything presumptuously...shall be cut off from among his people*" (Numbers 15:30 NKJV).

THE THIRD TEMPTATION: FORSAKING SPIRITUAL MEANS

Because of the Israelites' expectation of the sudden, spectacular appearance of the Messiah in the temple (see Malachi 3:1), the second temptation had a national aspect, whereas the temptation now before us, being associated with the kingdoms of this world, bears an international or universal distinction. Further, this was not another temptation of ambition, but rather to lower the standard of spiritual work by forsaking spiritual means; and so Jesus rejected it. This was not because He had no right to rulership over the world, but rather because the longer and harder way He was taking to become the King of Kings via the cross was the only right way to receive that rulership.

In effect, Satan said, "You want to control the world? Then take a shortcut—avoid the cross and accept the throne on easy terms. Do evil that good may come of it. Employ carnal weapons in spiritual warfare." But this grandiose and final approach, like the previous ones, signally failed in its design. "Evil had presented itself in disguise, making sins of distrust appear as acts of faith, while now it showed itself in its naked and absolute antagonism to the divine will."[34]

It may be fitting at this point to consider the authority with which Lucifer was originally invested by virtue of his seraphic origin—before he became the devil—and of which he boasted in his declared ownership of the kingdoms of this world. (See Matthew 4:8–9.) Luke, in his record of the wilderness experience of

---

34. Charles John Ellicott, ed., *The New Testament Commentary for Schools: St. Luke* (London: Cassell, Petter, Galpin & Co., 1880), 60–61.

Jesus, cited the devil as adding: *"all this authority...has been delivered to me, and I give it to whom I will"* (Luke 4:6). And the language of Jesus and that of His apostles appears to support this claim. Paul described him as *"the god of this world"* (2 Corinthians 4:4) and as *"the prince of the power of the air"* (Ephesians 2:2). As for his hosts, they are *"the world rulers of this present darkness"* (Ephesians 6:12). To Jesus, as we have seen, the devil was *"the ruler of this world"* (John 12:31; 14:30; 16:11). Jesus did not deny that the devil had the right to make such an offer in his third temptation, nor that he had the power to fulfill it. He simply refused to accept the rulership of the world on the devil's terms.

Again, when the world was originally created, Lucifer, as the devil was then known in his unfallen state, was granted the rulership of the world. With his rebellion, however, when he aspired to become like God, chaos overtook the original creation, and it became *"without form and void"* (Genesis 1:2) as the result of such a terrible catastrophe. Cosmos, however, came out of chaos to fit the creation for its new inhabitants and rulers. But, almost immediately, the enemy began his devilish work in the world. He could be restrained only by a superior power, which was promised in the first announcement of God's purpose in the incarnation of His Son. (See Genesis 3:14–15.)

We cannot doubt that, with his fall from heaven, the devil lost much of the glory and power of his angelic nature, and that, when he first commenced as the devil, God placed upon him chains of restraint as the badge of apostasy. He never possessed the divine attributes of omnipotence, omniscience, and omnipresence; and thus it was possible for God to place a general prohibition against him doing anything to the prejudice of creation or anything by force or violence without divine permission. Although the devil is the prince of demons, with hell at his command and with power as a roaring lion to devour, he is a lion locked up in the tower of the divine will; thus, he is unable to inflict the hurt he wishes or, indeed, any hurt at all. Through the victory Jesus secured over the devil in the wilderness, and by His death and resurrection, every child of God has the authority to challenge the devil's approach in temptation and say, "Get behind me, Satan!" and thereby overcome him.

All that the devil was originally granted was the *oversight* of the kingdoms of this world, not the *ownership* of them. But, true to his character as a deceiver, he offered Jesus as a gift something he did not own. Hezekiah distinctly declared, *"Thou art the God, thou alone, of all the kingdoms of the earth"* (2 Kings 19:15). As for David, he likewise affirmed, *"His kingdom rules over all"* (Psalm 103:19).

The devil, then, not only usurped his authority but reached the limit of his pride when, as an apostate angel, he not only offered Jesus ownership of a possession he did not own but also sought to persuade Him, the Lord of angels, to bow down and recognize him as a deity. Here was the devil of a god, seeking to induce the "very God of very God" (to use the words of the Nicene Creed) to become a devil worshipper! To have Jesus bow down and worship him would have been the masterstroke of his blasphemy.

As for the tempted One Himself, He could afford to despise the offer of the devil, for He knew that through His conquest of him, the kingdoms of this world would become His world-kingdom. (See Revelation 11:15.) The grand purpose of the incarnation was that Jesus should have an everlasting kingdom of grace and glory. "*Of his kingdom there will be no end*" (Luke 1:33). Ellicott's *Commentary* observes:

> The offer made by the Tempter rested upon the apparent evidence of the world's history. The rulers of the world, its Herods and its Caesars, seemed to have obtained their eminence by trampling the laws of God under foot, and accepting Evil as the Lord and Master of the World....In this case the temptation is no longer addressed to the sense of Sonship, but to the love of power. To be a king like other kings, mighty to deliver His people from their oppressors, and achieve the glory which the prophets had predicted for the Christ;—this was possible for Him if only He would go beyond the self-imposed limits of accepting whatsoever His Father ordered for Him.[35]

In His reply, Jesus "plucked the mask from the foe, who had assumed the fairest form to do the foulest deed" (to quote Bennett again) and commanded him to beat a hasty retreat—which he did, leaving Jesus for a season. "*Begone, Satan!*" Here Jesus used the most common alias, which is the devil's invariable name in the Old Testament, where it occurs some fifty times. *Satan*, as we have noted, means "adversary," and he has ever been the chief and persistent adversary of the written Word, of Jesus the Living Word, of the Father, and of the Holy Spirit. But this satanic Goliath met his defeat at the hand of David's Son and Lord, when Jesus used a single pebble from the brook of the Bible. Bennett continued:

> The Savior, having lifted up his heel...stamped upon the serpent; he that pretended to have worlds at his command, and to be able to promote

---

35. Ellicott, *New Testament Commentary for Schools: St. Luke*, 38.

Christ himself to honor, is now seen a poor vanquished, degraded foe, writhing under the foot of the conqueror. He who had defeated the First Adam, in the full strength of innocence, in Paradise, is himself conquered by the second, when starving in the desert.[36]

It will be observed that Jesus took no notice of the pomposity of the devil in vainly offering kingdoms for His homage. By His attitude, Jesus taught us that it is most dangerous to parley with temptation or to calculate apparent advantages that can be obtained only through unfaithfulness to the Lord our God. We also witness, in the rebuke of Jesus, His power over even the chief of the fallen angels by the powerful sword of the Spirit.

Jesus silenced the devil yet again by the quotation of another appropriate text. Again, His unfailing armory of defense in this contest and conquest was the divinely inspired Word of God. Three times over, He answered the devil with *"It is written."* He never argued or reasoned but simply quoted Scripture, for in its commands and counsels, precepts and promises, He had weapons of war mighty through God to the pulling down of the strongholds of the enemy. (See 2 Corinthians 10:4 KJV.) He defeated Satan by the means open to His humblest follower.

The apt Scripture that Jesus chose as His answer, and with which He parted with the devil, was from Deuteronomy 6:13. He said, *"You shall worship the Lord your God, and him only shall you serve"* (Matthew 4:10). What a crushing blow this dealt the tempter, who demanded that Jesus worship him, an apostate angel who, in his unfallen state, had worshipped God. Thus, the word *"worship"* used here emphasizes emphatically that what the tempter claimed was precisely what God had forbidden. As for the word *"only,"* does it not bring out most strongly the negative and prohibitory feature of the divine command? On the word *"serve,"* Jamieson noted that it is "never used by the LXX [Greek Old Testament] of any but religious service; and in this sense exclusively is it used in the New Testament, as we find it here."[37]

The Bible gave Jesus His light and answer, and so He bade Satan *"Begone."* He never looked for one moment at the delightful prospects the enemy presented but only at the dubious means. Jesus was resolved to go uncrowned as ruler of *"all the kingdoms"* until God crowned Him, and to employ no art but love to win the

36. Bennett, *Lectures*, 102.
37. Jamieson, *Commentary*, 25.

empire of mankind. Does His example not teach us that proper influence will come, if we deserve to have it, and that we should seek no power save that which naturally grows out of the consecrated service we are able to render for the spiritual benefit of others?

Was there not a sense in which the Man Christ Jesus facing Satan was *"the Lord your God"*? Was He not born as *"Christ the Lord"* (Luke 2:11); and did not Mary say of the holy Child she was about to bear, *"My soul magnifies the Lord, and my spirit rejoices in God my Savior"* (Luke 1:46–47)? As for being the object of worship, Jesus as God manifested in the flesh never refused it. The wise men fell down and worshipped Him when He was only a young child (see Matthew 2:11), unable to accept or refuse; but when He became a man, several are spoken of as worshipping Him during the three years of His public ministry. (See, for example, Matthew 8:2; 9:18; 15:25; 28:9, 28:17; Luke 19:37–40.) Thus, in effect, Jesus rebuked Satan by saying, "You blasphemously ask *Me* to worship *you*? Before your rebellion in heaven, you, along with the angelic host, worshipped Me as the Son of God, but when you transferred such worship to yourself, you corrupted your heart to the point where you could ask Me, as the Son of Man, to worship you. But demons and men alike must remember that I alone, as the Word made flesh, have the right to claim worship and adoration. You worship Me!"

A most important aspect of all three of our Lord's temptations that is essential to emphasize is that they were all external. As Professor Plummer expressed it:

> The change of scene is mental....The glory of all the kingdoms of the world could be suggested to the mind....What these words do imply is that the temptations came to Him from the outside. They were not the result, as many of our temptations are, of previous sin.[38]

There was nothing internal to which Satan could appeal. Satan could enter into Judas, seeing he already possessed a foothold in his traitorous heart. But the tempter could approach Jesus only from without, and so his temptations rebounded simply because there was no congenial soil in His sinless heart in which they could be planted and bear fruit. Jesus was internally and externally holy and conformed to the precepts of Scripture.

---

38. Alfred Plummer, *An Exegetical Commentary on the Gospel According to St. Matthew* (New York: Scribner's, 1910), 37.

As the Son of God, He left a sinless realm that was intrinsically holy, but as the Son of Man, He found Himself in a sinful world; still, during His sojourn on earth, He remained perfectly holy. The reason for this was the fact that He was born holy, that is, with no inherited evil propensities. In announcing Jesus' birth to Mary, the archangel Gabriel said, "*That holy thing which shall be born of thee shall be called the Son of God*" (Luke 1:35 KJV). Native sinfulness, or "original sin," was not inherited by Jesus, who, from His conception in Mary's womb to His death on the cross, remained "*holy, blameless, unstained, separated from sinners*" because He was "*exalted above the heavens*" (Hebrews 7:26).

Born with only a sinless nature, Jesus, tempted to the full as a Man, emerged from the conflict without sin, without being prompted to yield to the pressure of any evil nature within His assumed form. To His persistent, satanically inspired enemies, the Pharisees, He could say, "*Which of you convicts me of sin?*" (John 8:46). Peter wrote, "[Jesus] *committed no sin*" (1 Peter 2:22). Three times over, Pilate gave his verdict concerning the innocence of Jesus: "*I find no crime in this man*" (Luke 23:4; see verses 14, 22). Pilate's wife had troubling dreams about Jesus and urged her husband, "*Have nothing to do with that righteous man*" (Matthew 27:19). The scribes and Pharisees tempted Jesus over the woman taken in adultery who, if guilty, merited death by stoning. His pointed reply routed His foes: "*Let him who is without sin among you be the first to throw a stone at her*" (John 8:7). The only one present "*without sin*" was Jesus Himself, but He never raised a stone against the woman. Instead, He compassionately called her to holiness of life: "*Go, and do not sin again*" (John 8:11).

But with us, it is totally different, for we were "*brought forth in iniquity*" and "*conceived in sin.*" (See Psalm 51:5.) David's confession does not imply, as the ancient rabbis erroneously inferred, that he was born as the result of immorality, but rather represents a statement of the truth of experience, so constantly affirmed in Scripture, of hereditary corruption, the innate possession of every child of man. As we have noted, the temptations of Jesus, by contrast, were outward and ineffective, because there was nothing internal for them to rely upon.

As Francis Bacon wrote in his *Essays*, "It is not the lie that passeth through the mind, but the lie that sinketh in, and settleth in it, that doth the hurt." Because Jesus' heart was holy within, there was no lodgment there where the enemy's lies could settle. Was Jesus not most explicit about this when He said to His disciples, "*The prince of this world cometh, and hath nothing in me*" (John 14:30 KJV)? There was no territory within Him the devil could claim.

The temptation was a grim reality for Jesus, and He met the tempter in the strength of His sinless human nature, vitally assisted by divine grace. Because His heart was predisposed to obey the principles of Scripture, He could not be tempted at all. With us, however, the wiles of the devil receive a sympathetic consideration from the old nature we inherited and for which we are not responsible. Sin and condemnation come when we allow the devil to use this evil bent within for our spiritual defeat. Our deep depravity of nature is enough to make angels weep, but their sorrow is greater when we allow the devil to use it successfully to prevent holiness of life. Was not even Paul, who had known the Lord for many years and had even had a vision of the *"third heaven"* (2 Corinthians 12:2), conscious of this danger when he penned such verses as these? *"For I know that nothing good dwells within me, that is, in my flesh….If I do what I do not want, it is no longer I that do it, but sin which dwells within me….When I want to do right, evil lies close at hand"* (Romans 7:18, 20–21). The apostle, however, found a glorious deliverance from *"this body of death"* (verse 24) through *"Jesus Christ our Lord"* (verse 25). Jesus, then, had one nature, namely, a sinless nature; but the saints possess a dual nature—the old corrupt nature, condemned by God, and the new nature, received from the Holy Spirit in regeneration. Our responsibility is to have the new nature in the ascendancy and ever victorious over the old nature.

Matthew provided us with a striking conclusion to his account of our Lord's temptations: *"Then the devil left him, and behold, angels came…"* (Matthew 4:11). The devil; the angels! What extremes! Hell retreats; heaven appears!

Are you not arrested by the writer's *"Then"*? When was it that the devil left off harassing Jesus? Why, after he had exhausted all of his evil arts, for the time being. Luke put it this way: *"When the devil had ended all the* [every mode of] *temptation, he departed from him for a season"* (Luke 4:13 KJV). The devil found our Lord's third thrust of the sharp, two-edged sword so quick and powerful (see Hebrews 4:12) that, totally defeated, he left Him *"for a season,"* or until a further convenient occasion. He is never weary in his evildoing. Persistently and perseveringly, the devil pursues his prey in the hope of a final capture. As Bishop Jeremy Taylor remarked in his *Life and Death of the Holy Jesus*: "If he could ever have spied a time of returning, he wanted not will or malice to observe and use it."[39]

The contest was not finally over but renewed from time to time, as in Peter's insistence that Jesus would never suffer (see Matthew 16:22) and in the open

---

39. Antiquitates Christianae, or, *The History of the Life and Death of the Holy Jesus* (London: Flesher and Norton, 1678), 101.

enmity of the ruler of this world. The definite season here indicated was expressly referred to by Jesus: *"This is your hour, and the power of darkness"* (Luke 22:53). Calvary forever ended the satanic attacks upon Him, for His final cry—*"It is finished!"* (John 19:30 NKJV)—was the paean of absolute triumph over the devil and his angels.

THE ANGELS' MINISTRATION TO JESUS AFTER HIS TEMPTATION

"Behold, angels came." Truly, this was something to behold, for after the adversary came the angels! Hell had frowned, but now heaven smiled, succored, and refreshed the heart, and the strain of trial was more than repaired by its gracious ministries. Satan had tempted Jesus by the promise of angelic guardianship in a spectacular attempt to prove His messiahship. Now, legitimately, the promise was fulfilled on behalf of the victorious, yet weak and hungry, Son of Man. In addition to what we have already said regarding the ministry of angels, and to a following chapter devoted entirely to their relationship with Jesus, perhaps a further word is necessary as to their precise service at the conclusion of His temptations.

Poets and artists have depicted the angels serving Jesus a lavish banquet in the wilderness. Scripture leaves the nature of their ministration undefined. "What is instructive," said Ellicott, "is that the help of their service, the contrast between the calm and beauty of their presence and that of the wild beasts and of the tempter, comes as the reward of the abnegation which refused to make their ministry the subject of an experimental test." But the visit of the angels to the weary One must have been strengthening and encouraging, for Luke added, *"Jesus returned in the power of the Spirit into Galilee, and a report concerning him went out through all the surrounding country. And he taught in their synagogues, being glorified by all"* (Luke 4:14–15).

LESSONS FOR US FROM JESUS' TEMPTATION

What are some of the lessons for us to take to heart as we leave our absorbing meditation on the evident proof of our Lord's incarnation in His temptation? As we have already seen, Jesus refused to be relieved, even by a miracle, which He could have easily worked; but He continued to endure temptation rather than do what might indicate the least distrust of God. Timpson said in *The Angels of God*:

While we may, at any time, be tempted to seek relief unlawfully, or to violate duty for the sake of personal gratification, or the advantages of the world, we should remember our Savior, and cherish the unfeigned faith in the promises of God, which "are all yea and amen in Christ Jesus." We should ever hold fast by the written Word of His grace, assured that by the power of His Spirit, or the seasonable visitation of His angels, He will succor and deliver, and save us, even here on earth, and finally to His everlasting kingdom and glory!

This is how Jesus set for us the supreme example of resting on the Pillar of Incarnation. As the Son of God who came to earth as the Son of Man, He depended on "unfeigned faith in the promises of God," "the written Word of His grace," and "the power of His Spirit." We too may rely on these same provisions to lead a victorious life.

The uppermost lesson in the temptations, of course, is Jesus' use of Scripture, by which He resisted and overcame Satan. Scripture dwelt within Him richly in all wisdom, and His holy example and conquest in His trial teaches us that we can overcome the wicked one only as we are likewise vigilant and skillful in the use of Scripture. As Scripture is the inspired and infallible Word of God, may it have a constant home in our memories, affections, and hearts. Let us plead it in prayer, which God will notice, approve, and accept! The Holy Oracles are able to form, guide, and preserve right judgment; to curb, bound, and regulate our desires; to raise, confirm, and direct our expectations; to silence, enlighten, and purify our consciences; to convict and reprove sin and make us holy; and to make us daily overcomers when assailed by satanic forces.

3

THE PILLAR OF VINDICATION

"Vindicated in the Spirit...."
—1 Timothy 3:16

Before we enter the fascinating study of the five remaining brief poetic lines of this early confession of the Christian faith, it is important to examine their relative association with the great mystic secret revealed in the second clause, namely, the incarnation of the Son of God—that *God was manifested in the flesh!* The five impressive and progressive fragments of this triumph-song of the early churches, embracing, as they do, the leading facts of the messianic story, reinforce the assertion that Jesus was *"found in human form"* (Philippians 2:8), and they expand on His subsequent life and labors. The Gospels and the book of Acts describe in more detail each of the facets of Jesus' messianic career summarized here: the unfailing vindication by the Spirit of the character, conduct, and claims of Jesus during His days of humiliation; the beatific vision of the angels; the preaching of the cross; the glorious results of His sacrifice; and His return to heaven to the right hand of God. These are unassailable evidences of the truth that Jesus, as the Word, became flesh and dwelt among us. It is in the light of the incarnation, then, that we approach the remaining five lines of the ancient "confession-chant" (to adopt Dr. Arthur Way's term[40]) found in one of the greatest portions of Scripture, namely, 1 Timothy 3:16.

---

40. Arthur Way, *The Letters of St. Paul* (London: Macmillan, 1911), 202.

"By Spirit-power was He proved the Just One" is Way's translation of the statement we will now consider: *"He was...vindicated in the Spirit."* The Spirit's testimony to Jesus took place throughout His earthly sojourn, from His birth to His ascension, when, visibly, He left the earth as the God-Man. As the Spirit of Wisdom, the Holy Spirit was ever at the side of Christ, who came as *"the wisdom of God"* (1 Corinthians 1:24). The Spirit justified and substantiated all His affirmations and actions. There was the constant vindication of the Spirit against the gainsayers who objected to what Jesus claimed.

When He came among men, Jesus referred quite openly to the fact that He did not come into being at His birth but had always existed in *"the bosom of the Father"* (John 1:18). The *"beginning"* of John 1:1 goes back into eternity, long before the *"beginning"* of Genesis 1:1. Thus, Jesus' appearance as the holy Child was no afterthought with God. Did not Jesus declare that He came from the Father—that *"before Abraham was, I am"* (John 8:58)—an assertion His foes denied, and for which they tried to stone Him? Then we have the passages in which Jesus described Himself as *"he who descended from heaven"* (John 3:13); where He said, *"I proceeded and came forth from God"* (John 8:42); and where He spoke with the Father about *"the glory which I had with thee before the world was made"* (John 17:5). Jesus made a clear claim to preexistence.

Strange though it may seem, He received vindication for His claim to preexistence just *before* His birth. Prenatal vindication of this claim by the Spirit is to be found in the witness of Jesus' forerunner, John the Baptist. As we saw in chapter 1, John was miraculously born, much like the One whose way he came to prepare: his mother Elizabeth had not been able to have children and was beyond childbearing years when she conceived her illustrious son. (See Luke 1:5–13.) From his birth, John was filled with the Holy Spirit (see Luke 1:15); and by the same Spirit, he recognized Jesus when Mary came to visit his mother, and he *"leaped for joy"* in Elizabeth's womb. (See Luke 1:44.) Years later, when John came to baptize Jesus, he gave public testimony to what he had recognized about Him from the first: *"He who comes after me ranks before me, for he was before me"* (John 1:15). John, filled with the Spirit as always, thus upheld the truth that Jesus had lived before He was born in Bethlehem. The forerunner testified to Jesus as the One who had come from God, having dwelt in His bosom throughout the dateless past.

John also vindicated Jesus, based on the Spirit's witness, as the Son in whom God was well pleased. John reported that he had seen the Holy Spirit descending "*as a dove from heaven*" (John 1:32) and resting upon Jesus. Through this symbol, both the Spirit and John confirmed that the "*holy thing*" (Luke 1:35 kjv) born of Mary had lived a life of purity and peace throughout those thirty sinless, silent years in Nazareth. Scripture gives us only one glimpse of Jesus' perfect character during this period in which He grew to manhood, namely, the episode in the Jerusalem temple when He was only twelve years of age. His reply at that time to His agitated parents was most significant, seeing that it revealed the tenor of those hidden years: "*Did you not know that I must be about My Father's business?*" (Luke 2:49 nkjv).

The dove was also the emblem of the harmlessness and purity so characteristic of Jesus' brief but dynamic ministry of three years and of the peace He had come to provide for a restless, sinning world. No wonder John said, "*I have seen and have borne witness that this is the Son of God*" (John 1:34). God Himself declared, "*Thou art my beloved Son; in thee I am well pleased*" (Luke 3:22). What a wonderful dual justification of the One who could say, "*I always do what is pleasing to* [My Father]" (John 8:29)—a confession that inspired many of His listeners to believe in Him.

We would have thought that such a well-authenticated Person should have had the veneration, adoration, praise, and acceptance of all mankind. But no! In His humble home at Nazareth, before He faced the world, He was misunderstood by those around Him. He could say, in the words of the psalmist, "*I have become a stranger to my brethren, an alien to my mother's sons*" (Psalm 69:8). He was also something of an enigma to His mother and to His foster father, Joseph, as the temple episode shows. (See Luke 2:41–51.) He came to discharge a heaven-given task, but in His ministry, He endured three years of rejection, hatred, and humiliation from the religious leaders, as well as the animosity of hell. As "*the son of Mary*" (Mark 6:3), He did not occasion universal pleasure; but He had His Father's benediction, and nothing else mattered.

After denouncing cities that had spurned Him and His message, predicting they would be cast down to hell, and also conscious that "*serpents and scorpions*" (Luke 10:19) were combined to hurt Him, nevertheless "*in that same hour* [Jesus] *rejoiced in the Holy Spirit*" (verse 21). Weymouth translated the passage in this way: "*Jesus was filled by the Holy Spirit with rapturous joy.*" Another rendering is, "He was thrilled with joy at that hour in the Holy Spirit." Thus, the Spirit was not only our Lord's justifier but also the source of His joy, enabling Him to triumph over His circumstances and to glory even in His tribulations. "*Anointed...*

with the oil of gladness" (Hebrews 1:9), He possessed an inward peace and tran-
quility independent of all outward experiences and happiness.

In spite of those who did not believe in Jesus, the Holy Spirit could say
"Amen!" to all His claims to divine sonship. But, at the same time, as Peter
reminded us, *"the Spirit of Christ…testified beforehand the sufferings of Christ, and
the* [vindicating] *glory that should follow"* (1 Peter 1:11 KJV). The Spirit knew that
this Man who received sinners and ate and drank with them would experience
weariness, need of sleep, hunger, thirst, pain, soul trouble, agony of mind and
body, tears, sorrow, shame, contempt, scourging, physical torture, and death. The
same Spirit who justified Jesus' claims to deity, which He made often in the days
of His humiliation, also amply vindicated His sinlessness and His willingness
to bear all suffering without retaliation. *"When he was reviled, he did not revile
in return; when he suffered, he did not threaten"* (1 Peter 2:23). The marvel of the
gospel is that *"by his wounds you have been healed"* (verse 24). This is the divine
example we are to emulate. (See verse 21.) The Divine Vindicator knew that this
much-tried Man, amid all of His trials and sufferings, would declare the possession of a heart at peace with God and assure His followers, who would follow in
His steps in suffering, *"Peace I leave with you; my peace I give to you"* (John 14:27).

The most outstanding, wonderful, and triumphant evidence of the Spirit's
justification of the life, work, and death of Jesus, however, was the resurrection,
for which the Spirit was responsible. Paul said that Jesus was *"designated Son of
God in power according to the Spirit of holiness by his resurrection from the dead"*
(Romans 1:4). Indeed, with united voice, the New Testament affirms that the
Holy Spirit was "the efficient cause" of our Lord's victory over the grave. Peter said
that He was *"put to death in the flesh, but quickened by the Spirit"* (1 Peter 3:18 KJV).
As the Spirit of Life, the Holy Spirit made possible the conception of Jesus and
also the resurrection of Jesus. As in the virgin womb of Mary the Spirit fashioned
the physical body of Jesus, so in the virgin tomb of Joseph of Arimathea He fashioned the glorified body of Jesus. The Roman authorities fixed their official seal
on the outside of the tomb, assuring that Jesus would not rise again; but God set
His seal—the Spirit—within the tomb as evidence that Jesus would rise again
and not *"see corruption"* (Psalm 16:10 KJV, NKJV).

Thus, the Spirit who gave the prenatal life and brought it to birth was the
same Spirit who quickened our Lord's dead body and brought Him forth as the
"first begotten of the dead" (Revelation 1:5 KJV). The Spirit not only gave life to
a corpse but "reunited the human spirit to its proper dwelling, not as a mere

tenement, but as a home, insusceptible of further death."[41] What a glorious vindication this was of all the previous claims of Jesus! Ellicott's *Commentary* says:

> The truth of Jesus Christ's own assertion respecting Himself...in the end was triumphantly vindicated....It was by His resurrection from the dead that Christ's lofty claims to the Godhead were justified....In the power of this Spirit, which He had within Himself, He did take His life which He had laid down, did re-unite His soul unto His body from which He separated it when He gave up the ghost, and so did quicken and revive Himself, and thus publicly proclaimed His divine nature, His awful dignity.[42]

In all this, therefore, Jesus left us an example that we should follow in His steps. As His followers, we should know what it is to be dead to self-vindication, awaiting at all times the Spirit's justification, which, sooner or later, is given, much to the confusion of those who misjudge us. There is a difference between reputation and character. *Reputation* is what others think and say about us. *Character* is what we actually are. As D. L. Moody used to say, "Character is what a man is in the dark." Jesus cared not about His reputation but flung it to the winds and *"made himself of no reputation"* (Philippians 2:7 KJV). As to His character, it was perfect, for even Pilate confessed, *"I find no crime in this man"* (Luke 23:4). If, in our hidden heart, God is fully and obediently acknowledged and the Spirit of Joy is in possession of our being, then we can be confident that, sooner or later, our true character will be vindicated, whatever ups and downs our reputation may experience in the meantime. This, then, is the Pillar of Vindication: to wait quietly and patiently for the Spirit's justification, with the same confidence that Jesus, our example, has modeled for us.

---

41. Arthur Cleveland Downer, *The Mission and Ministration of the Holy Spirit* (Edinburgh: T. & T. Clark, 1909), 58–59.
42. Ellicott, *New Testament Commentary for Schools: St. Luke*, 225.

4

THE PILLAR OF REVELATION

"Seen by angels...."
—1 Timothy 3:16

Things into which angels long to look" (1 Peter 1:12). That is how the apostle Peter described the *"sufferings of Christ and the subsequent glory"* (verse 11) about which the prophets spoke centuries beforehand, which they *"searched and inquired"* (verse 10) to understand. The attitude Peter ascribed to the angels implies a distinct apprehension of the wonder and purpose of the incarnation. It is reminiscent of the cherubim and seraphim bending over the mercy seat in the tabernacle of old. At each end of the mercy seat was a winged cherub, beaten out of pure gold. The faces of the two cherubim were turned toward one another, and their bodies were placed in an attitude of bending over the ark, as if with an earnest desire to look into the mysteries hidden under its golden lid. This same gaze is what Peter emphasized when he used the Greek term *parakupto*, "to look into," literally, "to bend aside to see." The word implies a strained attention to something that catches the eye somewhat out of its usual line of sight. The term is used in the Gospels for those who bent down to look into Jesus' tomb (see Luke 24:12 KJV, NKJV; John 20:5), and it aptly expresses the eagerness of the angels to see and understand what God was preparing for the salvation of humanity.

But as Paul told us in the passage that serves as the basis of our meditation in this book, the angels did not just long to look into these things; they actually *saw* them—"*He was...seen by angels.*" And they not only saw them but also testified about them, just like the apostles who told the council, "*We cannot but speak of what we have seen and heard*" (Acts 4:20). Indeed, the angels were God's chosen messengers to testify to the significance of each phase of Jesus' life on earth:

+ the preparations for His coming
+ His birth
+ His temptation
+ His teachings
+ His sufferings
+ His resurrection
+ His ascension

Through their presence and their proclamation at each of these times, they revealed the divine purposes that were at work when the Son of God came to earth as the Son of Man.

The book of Hebrews calls the old covenant "*the message declared by angels*" (Hebrews 2:2). Paul said similarly that the law was "*ordained by angels*" (Galatians 3:19). There is a sense, as we will discover in this chapter, in which the new covenant is also "*the message declared by angels,*" since angels testified to God's purposes during each phase of Jesus' life. But, as the book of Hebrews goes on to explain, in a much greater way, the new covenant was "*declared at first by the Lord, and it was attested to us by those who heard him, while God also bore witness by signs and wonders and various miracles and by gifts of the Holy Spirit*" (Hebrews 2:3–4). The divine purposes originally revealed through the angels, and then declared by the Lord, to which God bore witness, have now also received inspired apostolic attestation in the Scriptures. And that is how this next phrase in the "confession-chant," "*seen by angels,*" constitutes the Pillar of Revelation: We may rest in confident faith on what was revealed about Jesus through the original angelic witness, now recorded for us in the scriptural accounts of these same events.

Let us now explore what the four Gospels tell us about how the angels revealed God's purposes throughout the life and labors of the preexistent One who was manifested in a human form, in each of the significant phases of His life that we have already summarized.

ANGELS AND DIVINE PREPARATIONS FOR THE BIRTH OF CHRIST

The earliest reference to an angel in the New Testament story comes in Luke's account of the divine preparations for Jesus' birth. Luke explained how an angel of the Lord, identified as Gabriel, foretold the birth of John the Baptist, who would prepare the way for the appearance of the long-promised Messiah. Gabriel came to a couple named Zechariah and Elizabeth, who were persons of singular piety, being *"righteous before God,"* and practiced in spiritual loveliness, for both walked *"in all the commandments and ordinances of the Lord blameless"* (Luke 1:6). Both were also well advanced in years. Tradition has it that Elizabeth was eighty-nine years of age, and that Zechariah was a few years older than his wife.

While Zechariah was engaged in his sacred duty as a priest at the altar, this celestial messenger stood near; and, seeing him, Zechariah was afraid. The majestic stranger, however, quickly announced his mission: *"Do not be afraid, Zechariah, for your prayer is heard, and your wife Elizabeth will bear you a son, and you shall call his name John"* (Luke 1:13). Venturing a reply, the priest pointed out the natural impossibility of such an unexpected promise, seeing his wife had been unable to bear children, and seeing that she was now very aged. And so Zechariah asked the angel, *"How shall I know this?"* (Luke 1:18)—that the birth of a son would be a reality? In response, he received a most unexpected sign, namely, temporary muteness. Elizabeth, on the other hand, believed the gracious word of the Lord that the angel had announced. At the appointed time, she conceived and rejoiced gratefully, *"Thus the Lord has done to me in the days when he looked on me, to take away my reproach among men"* (Luke 1:25). Thus, like Isaac, who was born to Abraham and Sarah when they were very old (see Genesis 21:1–2), John was miraculously conceived. As we saw in chapter 1, both Elizabeth and Mary learned that *"with God nothing will be impossible"* (Luke 1:37).

With the birth of John, the speech of his righteous father was restored. Filled with the Holy Spirit, he said of his son, who was filled with the same Spirit from his birth:

> You, child, will be called the prophet of the Most High; for you will go before the Lord to prepare his ways, to give knowledge of salvation to his people in the forgiveness of their sins, through the tender mercy of our God, when the day shall dawn upon us from on high to give light to those who sit in darkness and in the shadow of death, to guide our feet into the way of peace.　(Luke 1:76–79)

As for John himself, when the time came for him to appear to Israel, this extraordinary child, now a young man, commissioned by the Spirit of God, preached that he was only *"the voice...crying in the wilderness"* (John 1:23), calling upon the people to repent and be baptized. He explained that although he baptized the repentant in water, One would soon come after him who would baptize *"with the Holy Spirit and with fire"*; he said that this coming One *"is mightier than I..., the thong of whose sandals I am not worthy to untie"* (Luke 3:16). John had the sacred privilege of baptizing Jesus in the Jordan, and also of being the first martyr for declaring the mission of the Savior, whose way he had prepared. Jesus Himself declared, *"Among those born of women there has risen no one greater than John the Baptist"* (Matthew 11:11).

The first appearance of Gabriel, then, who is the only heavenly messenger to be named in the Gospels, was of the utmost significance, for he not only declared the name that Zechariah and Elizabeth should call their illustrious son—*"You shall call his name John"* (Luke 1:13)—but also announced that the Babe to be born shortly after John was the Lord God of the children of Israel (see Luke 1:16)—God manifested in the flesh for their salvation. Thus, the early preparation for the coming of the God-Man so clearly foretold by Gabriel, the angelic spokesman for God, indicated divine fidelity and grace.

Angelic activity continued as the preparations for the birth of Jesus then came to include His mother, Mary. Devout hearts preparing to meditate upon the unique ministry of angels in connection with the birth of our beloved Savior realize the necessity of approaching such a solemn theme in reverence and in godly fear, for the place whereon they stand is holy ground. Virginity of heart is necessary, if our finite mind is to grasp the great mystery of our Christian faith, namely, Christ's miraculous birth to the Virgin Mary. The fact of Him, by His birth, becoming Immanuel, or *"'Emmanuel' (which means, God with us)"* (Matthew 1:23), involving, as it did, the incarnation of Deity, the personal union of the Godhead with a human infant, is far above the comprehension of the loftiest intellect of man, and perhaps even of the angels themselves.

What a comforting truth this is to carry with us through the day, that God is with us, God in our bodily form for our sole consolation. Jesus came with the nature of His Father; hence, He has the ability to be our everyday Friend, checking our fears and sympathizing with us in our sorrows. He has also our nature; hence, He is able to meet our needs and cause all things to work together for our good. Jesus is God with us—in us—for us! So, take courage: the ear of your

Immanuel is ever open; the heart of your Immanuel is ever tender; the arm of your Immanuel is ever strong. We must clearly understand that there was a Man of two natures, the divine and the human, in the Person of our Lord Jesus Christ. It is a point of the deepest importance. We should settle it firmly in our minds that our Savior is perfect Man, as well as perfect God. The name *Immanuel* takes in the whole mystery.

Jesus was to come of "the seed of the woman" (see Genesis 3:15), not of man; this promise was fulfilled when He was conceived by the Holy Spirit and born of the Virgin Mary. Thus, by the manner of His conception, the holiness of His nature was secured and His fitness to be the Savior of a sinful world assured to all mankind. Man only is the product of natural generation; but *"the man Christ Jesus"* (1 Timothy 2:5), born of the Virgin, was *"that holy thing"* (Luke 1:35 kjv), the Son of God—composed of a pure and unpolluted humanity in the temple of deity. As we noted in chapter 1, reason may find this hard to accept. But, as Malcolm Muggeridge said:

> To a twentieth-century mind the notion of a virgin birth is intrinsically and preposterously inconceivable. If a woman claims—such claims are made from time to time—to have become pregnant without sexual inter-course, no one believes her. Yet for centuries millions upon millions of people never doubted that Mary had begotten Jesus without the partici-pation of a husband or lover. Nor was such a belief limited to the simple and unlettered; the most profound and most erudite minds, the greatest artists and craftsmen, found no difficulty in accepting the Virgin birth as an incontestable fact—for instance, Pascal, who in the versatility of his gifts and the originality of his insights was regarded as the Aristotle of his time.[43]

Are we, then, to suppose that our forebears who believed implicitly in the virgin birth were gullible fools?

Mary herself was of the royal house of David, and although she was young, she was one of the many who *"were looking for the redemption of Jerusalem"* (Luke 2:38). But what a soul-moving revelation and experience it must have been when she learned from the angel Gabriel, this heavenly visitant who hon-ored her by addressing her by her proper name, that she was to be the mother of the glorious Redeemer. Calmed by the beaming benevolence of Gabriel,

43. Muggeridge, *Jesus: The Man Who Lives*, 19.

Mary spoke to him with unaffected modesty, holy meekness, and rational piety, as the seraphic messenger satisfied her inquiries and removed all her scruples.

> *Said Mary unto the angel, How shall this be, seeing I know not a man? And the angel answered and said unto her, The Holy Ghost shall come upon thee, and the power of the Highest shall overshadow thee: therefore also that holy thing which shall be born of thee shall be called the Son of God.*
>
> (Luke 1:34–35 KJV)

Gabriel not only uttered Mary's name as he announced the birth of her Son but also told her what she should name Him: *"You shall call his name Jesus"* (Luke 1:31). Does this not prove how intimately the angels, as ministering spirits, are familiar with all the circumstances of the people of God? Without doubt, Jesus is the sweetest name on mortal tongue and is, in the words of the hymn "The Name of Jesus Is So Sweet":

> That name I fondly love to hear,
> It never fails my heart to cheer,
> Its music dries a falling tear;
> Exalt the name of Jesus.

It is most appropriate that Luke should have been chosen to record the delicate, intimate aspects of the conception and birth of Jesus, for, as *"the beloved physician"* (Colossians 4:14) and a believer, he was well qualified to set forth those things that were *"delivered to us by those who from the beginning were eyewitnesses and ministers of the word"* (Luke 1:2). Joseph Hall wrote in his *Contemplations*:

> The Spirit of God was never so accurate in any description as that, which concerns the incarnation of God. It was fit no circumstance should be omitted in that story, whereon the faith, and salvation, of all the world dependeth. We cannot so much as doubt of this truth, and be saved. No, not the number of the month, not the name of the angel, is concealed. Every particle imports not more certainty, than excellence.... The Messenger is an angel. A man was too mean to carry the news of the conception of God. Never any business was conceived in heaven, that did so much concern the earth, as the Conception of the God of heaven in Womb of Earth. No less than an archangel was worthy to bear

this tidings; and never any angel received a greater honor, than of this embassage.[44]

We might add that never any man received a greater honor than Luke did when he was guided by the Spirit to write out in order all that the celestial messenger had declared to Zechariah, Elizabeth, and Mary. This is why Luke's gospel presents Jesus as the human-divine One, just as John reveals Him as the divine-human One. Jesus, as the Son of God who became the Son of Man, is the keynote of Luke's wonderful record.

It may be fitting at this point to emphasize that among the multitudes of the angelic army around the throne of God, only two of the angels who did not rebel with Lucifer are specifically named—Michael and Gabriel, both of whom are archangels, that is, among the first rank of angels, and who were given the most important missions on earth to fulfill. A comparison of the two is interesting. The name *Michael* means "Who is like God?" Thus, he has a name suggesting self-oblation, self-obliteration. He never gloried in himself. He would not rebuke the devil but left him to the Lord. (See Jude 1:9.) *The Book of Enoch*, a traditional Jewish work, extols his meekness, calling him "the merciful, the patient, the holy Michael." In the book of Daniel, he is named as *"one of the chief princes"* (Daniel 10:13) of the nation of Israel, and as *"the great prince who has charge of your people"* (Daniel 12:1). He is also mentioned twice in the New Testament, in both cases contending with the devil. (See Jude 1:9; Revelation 12:7.) Gabriel, whose name means "the strength of God" or "the hero of God," appears fewer times than his fellow archangel. He had two missions to Daniel (see Daniel 8:16; 9:21) and then his missions to Zechariah and Mary. His was the greatest privilege any angel ever had, seeing that he was chosen to proclaim the birth of Jesus.

A comparison of these holy two reveals Michael to be the champion who fought the battles of faith and who was ever on the side of his God. He it was who overcame the evil, satanic prince of Persia; and his great celestial and militant hosts are the seraphs who warred against the devil and his angels. As for Gabriel, he is not referred to as having contact with the devil. There is in his manifestation a simplicity and absence of terror corresponding to his character as comforter. He is the angel who wrote down divine decrees, the angelic prophet, interpreter of the prophetic Word, revealer of the purposes of God, sent to man in the form of a man before God sent His Son to take human form.

44. Joseph Hall, *The Works of Joseph Hall*, vol. 2, *Contemplations* (London: Whittingham, 1808), 200.

To return to Mary herself, even though she was deeply affected by the appearance and announcement of Gabriel, and pondered his words about her aged cousin Elizabeth, she was anxious to ascertain the truth of the miraculous event she expected, and so she *"arose and went with haste into the hill country,…* *and she entered the house of Zechariah and greeted Elizabeth"* (Luke 1:39–40). Now Elizabeth must have been overwhelmed as her youthful, virgin cousin recounted the marvelous communication of Gabriel! To quote Bishop Hall again: "Only the meeting of saints in heaven can parallel the meeting of these two cousins; the two wonders of the world are met under one roof and congratulate their mutual happiness."[45]

The remarkable, Spirit-inspired benediction of Elizabeth, *"Blessed are you among women, and blessed is the fruit of your womb!"* (Luke 1:42), was a most apt expression of devout praise, revealing Mary's humility, faith, and privilege! What deep joy must have been Elizabeth's as her longed-for babe leaped in her womb while in Mary's presence (Luke 1:41)—"a sympathetic emotion of the unconscious babe, at the presence of Mary the mother of his Lord."[46] What a remarkable phrase Elizabeth used in her sincere, heartfelt congratulation: *"Why is this granted me, that the mother of my Lord should come to me?"* (Luke 1:43). Olshausen observed:

> Turn this as we will, we shall never be able to see the propriety of calling an unborn child "Lord," but by supposing Elizabeth, like the prophets of old, enlightened to perceive the Messiah's Divine nature.[47]

As for Mary, influenced by the same heavenly inspiration as her aged cousin, she burst forth in expressions of exalting joy, which revealed her richly furnished and devout mind. Her *Magnificat* (Luke 1:46–55) is "a magnificent canticle, in which the strain of Hannah's ancient song, in like circumstances, is caught up, and just slightly modified and sublimed."[48] The statement that stands out in her tribute to Him who had done great things for her is the one in which she confessed that the Babe she was to bear would be her Savior, as well as the Savior of the world: *"My soul magnifies the Lord, and my spirit rejoices in God my Savior"* (Luke 1:46–47). The terms *"my soul"* and *"my spirit"* imply *"all that is within me"* (Psalm 103:1). An immaculate life was evidently hers; otherwise, God would not

---

45. Hall, *Contemplations*, 277.
46. Jamieson, *Commentary*, 244.
47. Quoted in Jamieson, *Commentary*, 245.
48. *Commentary*, 245.

have chosen her—a virgin—to be a mother. Yet she voiced her need of the salvation her Son would provide, and generations have called her blessed for such a confession. (See Luke 1:48.)

As we conclude our consideration of the role of angels in revealing God's purposes during the preparations for Jesus' birth, we turn to Joseph, who, discovering that Mary was *"found to be with child"* (Matthew 1:18), was overwhelmed and dreading the shame that must unavoidably cover one who had been so dear to him. In his perplexity, he sought direction from God, for he knew that in cases of infidelity on the part of a *"betrothed virgin,"* the law of God required divorcement, denouncing, and a terrible punishment of death by stoning. (See Deuteronomy 22:23–24.) Graciously, God answered Joseph's plea through the ministry of an angel. (See Matthew 1:20.) Later, through the same angelic agency, Joseph was instructed to flee into Egypt and then, at a safe time, to return. (See Matthew 2:13, 19–20.)

It does not appear as if Mary had made known to Joseph her peculiar circumstances. Probably, she left her cause and reputation to her covenant God, and the angelic visit Joseph received rewarded her confidence and faith by causing every vestige of doubt to vanish from his upright and candid mind, in relation to the virtue of his espoused wife. Timpson, in his incomparable study on *The Angels of God*, ended his chapter on the Virgin Mary with this unique tribute to Joseph:

> Mary's unspotted purity being thus established by the special testimony of heaven—in perfect accordance with the statement which must have been made by Mary herself, as to the visit of the angel Gabriel—the servant of God made no hesitation in obeying the Divine command, following the dictates of his own benevolent heart....While we admire the merciful condescension of God towards the Virgin Mary, in the mission of the angel Gabriel, we behold in Joseph a fine example of gentleness and prudence. He was careful to avoid any precipitate steps; and in the critical moments of his anxious deliberation, God, who knew his uprightness and singleness of heart, graciously interposed to guide and determine his resolutions. Joseph's decision, in taking Mary to his own home, when satisfied by the assurance of the angel of the Lord, was worthy of his reputation for piety, and it affords to us an instructive pattern of prompt obedience, whenever our duty may call us to glory our God and Savior.

ANGELS AT THE BIRTH OF JESUS

Let us now consider the role of angels in revealing God's purposes at the time of the actual birth of Jesus. What a jubilant day it was for the angelic hierarchy of heaven when they gazed upon the face of the newborn King! In Luke 2:8–14, when the *"angel,"* perhaps Gabriel, made his announcement to the pious, poor shepherds, the *"multitude of the heavenly host"* accompanying this angel became happy songsters and formed themselves into a celestial chorus to praise God. The birth of the babe was *"good news of a great joy,"* not only *"to all the people,"* but also to the angelic legions as they beheld

> human nature so highly exalted, and that God was man, and man was God; they were transported with admiration…seeing God so humbled, and man so changed, and so full of charity, that God stooped to the condition of man, and man was inflamed beyond the love of seraphim, and was made more knowing than cherubim, more established than thrones, more happy than all the orders of angels.[49]

Although they did sing then, as angels alone can sing, the song of redemption was one in which they could not join, because it is, in the words of the hymn "There's a Friend for Little Children":

> A song which even angels
> Can never, never sing:
> They know not Christ as Savior,
> But worship Him as King.

While the angels are blessed to surround the throne of God, theirs will never be the privilege of saints to share His throne—*"He who conquers, I will grant him to sit with me on my throne"* (Revelation 3:21). Let us try to appreciate, however, the happy welcome with which the angels introduced Jesus to a sinful and sinning world.

The first impressive feature of the birth narratives is the marked contrast apparent in their joint accounts of the greatest event in world history: Envision the comparison between the angel's humble audience and the dazzling glory of the Lord, which characteristically encompassed heavenly visions and visitations—and

---

49. Jeremy Taylor, *The Whole Works of the Right Rev. Jeremy Taylor* (London: Westley and Davis, 1835), I:46.

this was the angelic revelation of the greatest tidings ever published abroad, the seraphic serenaders proclaiming the shortest, greatest sermon ever preached! What honored company did Gabriel address? Was it the proud Roman, Herod, "the King of the Jews," "the Master of the World," and his haughty nobles living in luxurious significance in their stately mansions? Or did the blessed angel hasten to the priests and Levites guarding the sacred finest in the temple? No, the message came to the most insignificant persons—but for a reason.

The Babe the angels praised came not to be king. He was born a King, but no worldly pomp awaited the approach of this heavenly King—no flourish of trumpets heralded the event, no palace was built to receive Him, no purple robes were ready for His adornment. The beauty of this greatest story ever told is that the poor but pious shepherds, who, as they watched their flocks at night, doubtless meditated upon the ancient Scripture prophesying that the Messiah would come as the Good Shepherd, were the first to receive the good tidings the angel brought from heaven. These shepherds, along with other devout Jews, waited for the redemption of Israel; and their reward came when the darkness of one night was filled with splendor, and their night was turned to day—symbolic of the spiritual mission of Him who had come as the Light of the World. But if the shepherds were the first to receive news of His birth and also the first to see Jesus, the sages from afar had the next sight of the newborn King. It is "even so, still simplicity first, science next, finds its way to Christ."[50] In the words of John Keble's hymn "What Sudden Blaze of Song":

> Thee, on the bosom laid
> Of a pure virgin mind,
> In quiet ever, and in shade,
> Shepherd and sage may find;
> They, who have bowed untaught to Nature's sway,
> And they, who follow Truth along her star-paved way.

The sign given the devout and lowly shepherds that the divine announcement was authentic was that the Babe would be found in a manger when they went to Bethlehem to *"see this thing that has happened, which the Lord has made known to us"* (Luke 2:15). Coming from the spaciousness and splendor of the Father's house, with its many mansions, the Babe found no royal nursery with a beautifully prepared crib to receive Him, even though a winged seraph from the

---

50. Jamieson, *Commentary*, 99.

court of heaven had been commissioned to announce His birth. No palace or noble mansion was open to welcome Joseph and Mary, even though they were of a royal family and singly honored by the King Eternal. Being poor, they were not financially able to procure desirable accommodations, not even within the small wayside inn, so that Mary could have the privacy her delicate condition required.

John reminds us that Jesus *"came to his own home, and his own people received him not"* (John 1:11). Well, He certainly came to His own world, which He had created; but there was no room, even in the modest inn, for Him. Therefore, His godly mother was forced to endure the humiliating necessity of bringing forth her firstborn in a stable, and to have for His cradle a manger or crib or stall, in which food for animals was placed. What a humiliation for both mother and Babe—especially for the Babe who came as the Lord of glory manifested in flesh. Keble also has a stanza on this grim experience:

> Wrapped in His swaddling bands,
> And in His manger laid,
> The Hope and Glory of all lands
> Is come to the world's aid:
> No peaceful home upon his cradle smiled,
> Guests rudely went and came, where slept the royal Child.

God, however, had sent His own illustrious visitors to pay court to Him who was to say to Pilate, as He came to die, *"You say that I am a king. For this I was born, and for this I have come into the world"* (John 18:37). The contrast between the glorious descriptions given Him at His birth and the conditions He would be found in is overpowering. He whose *"goings forth have been from of old, from everlasting"* (Micah 5:2 KJV) would be seen as a Babe in the crib of oxen. He whom the heaven of heavens could not contain (see 1 Kings 8:27; 2 Chronicles 2:6; 6:18) would be discovered *"wrapped in swaddling clothes and lying in a manger"* (Luke 2:12)—a mystery angels desired to look into.

Paul seemed to have had these amazing contrasts, which were Christ's chosen style, in mind when he wrote, *"Though he was rich, yet for your sake he became poor, so that by his poverty you might become rich"* (2 Corinthians 8:9). "He became poor." As the preexistent One, the Lord of glory and of angels, this beloved Son dwelt in the bosom of the Father, but He became *poor*, so very poor, for He came as the Son of another man's spouse, was born in another man's abode, dined at another man's table, slept in another man's boat, rode on another man's donkey, and was buried in another man's grave. Truly, He sounded the depths of humiliation for our sakes! "So that by His poverty we might become rich": yes, enriched beyond measure, with riches of His grace and mercy here and now and in the life to come, the riches of glory as our eternal inheritance.

Looking again at the birth narrative as given by Luke, several aspects of the angelic visitation that accompanied this glorious event, and of the angel's heavenly message, stand out prominently. The first is the *angelic courier*. A courier is described by the dictionary as an "express messenger," and this is how the angel functioned when he appeared to the shepherds who were overawed and frightened by the glory of the Lord enveloping them. *"Be not afraid"* (Luke 2:10), said the courier, who was heaven's express messenger to the faithful shepherds. Then there followed the message heaven had commissioned him to deliver—*"Behold, I bring you good news of a great joy which will come to all the people"* (Luke 2:10)—a declaration of the universality of the gospel. The qualifying terms *"good"* and *"great"* indicate the nature of the gospel itself. Salvation for a lost world was surely the greatest, most joyous news mankind has ever received. Isaac Watts summarized this news in his hymn "Join All the Glorious Names":

> By Thee the joyful news
> Of our salvation came,
> The joyful news of sin forgiv'n,
> Of hell subdued and peace with heav'n.

Another prominent aspect of the angel's message was its indication of the *time and place* of the Savior's birth. Traditionally, we celebrate December 25 as the natal day of Jesus. Many Bible scholars, however, believe His birthday was a few days later, very early in January. While we may never know the exact date of His birth, the fact that matters is that He was "born to give man second birth." When the angel said, *"To you is born this day...a Savior"* (Luke 2:11), he was speaking of the very day when the Word was made flesh.

The specification of His place of birth was just as significant. The inspired prediction required that the Messiah should be born in Bethlehem, as the advent song of Micah made clear: *"But you, O Bethlehem Ephrathah, who are little to be among the clans of Judah, from you shall come forth for me one who is to be ruler in Israel, whose origin is from of old, from ancient days"* (Micah 5:2). Prophecy directed Israel where to look for Him, and their faith accordingly expected Him. At the time when Christ was born, the whole

Sanhedrin identified Bethlehem as the birthplace of the expected Messiah. (See Matthew 2:4–6.)

But, somehow, little attention has been given to God's overruling providence, which caused Jesus to come of the right line—the house of David—and at the right place—the City of David. Without these historic moorings of our faith, substantial Christianity would be lost. Gabriel's visitation to Mary took him to Nazareth, where she dwelt; but the angel's appearance to the shepherds to announce the birth of Him who was conceived by the Spirit in Nazareth found him in Bethlehem, some one hundred miles from Nazareth.

While Joseph and Mary doubtless knew of Micah's prophecy about Bethlehem being the birthplace of Jesus, they remained in their usual abode in Nazareth. How, then, did the unexpected, slow, and arduous journey, particularly for Mary, come about? Behind such we see how God can make the most unlikely events subservient to the accomplishment of His designs, as Timpson suggested in *The Angels of God*:

> The vanity of a heathen monarch, in a distant country, was overruled to bring about the completion of the Divine purposes: for Augustus Cesar, the Roman Emperor, is allowed to "set his unwieldy empire in motion, from the Baltic to the Atlantic, and from Britain, or Gaul, to the extremity of Egypt and Syria" for this purpose. He issued, therefore, an edict for a census of all his subjects to be made; and the enrollment of the whole population of Canaan required that the inhabitants of Judah, though living in distant towns, should register themselves in the places of their original family inheritances (Luke 2:1–4). Hence Joseph and Mary, at the momentous period, being of the royal "house and lineage," though greatly reduced in circumstances, repaired to Bethlehem, the City of David, for the necessary registration. Infinite wisdom arranged the whole plan for the advent of the great Messiah.

The names and titles given to Jesus are another striking feature of the angel's message. Joseph and Mary were spared the problem of having to choose the most fitting name for their Child, because His name had already been chosen for Him by heaven. The angel who appeared to Joseph in a dream told him, *"You shall call his name Jesus, for he will save his people from their sins"* (Matthew 1:21), and Gabriel told Mary similarly, *"You shall call his name Jesus"* (Luke 1:31). We are therefore not surprised to read, at the end of this birth account, that *"he was called Jesus, the name given by the angel before he was conceived in the womb"* (Luke 2:21). But beyond this given name, there are the three titles the angel announced, namely, *"Savior," "Christ,"* and *"Lord."* (See Luke 2:11.) What marvelous, imperishable titles these are!

Savior! The angelic bearer of this God-given name did not speak to the shepherds of "one who shall be a Savior," but of One who was "born a Savior," implying that He was such before He was born. According to His own teaching, Jesus came *"to seek and to save the lost"* (Luke 19:10) and not essentially, as some would claim, to be a great social reformer, a great teacher, a great philanthropist, or a great martyr who died for the truth he believed in. In a way, He was all these things, but the Scripture looks at Jesus only as the world's Redeemer, who was born and who died to save sinners.

Christ—Lord! The angel paired these names together, saying, *"who is Christ the Lord"* (Luke 2:11). Dean Alford said of this magnificent appellation, "This is the only place where these words come together; and I see no way of understanding this 'Lord' but as corresponding to the Hebrew JEHOVAH."[51] Aged Simeon was assured by the Holy Spirit that he would not die until he had seen *"the Lord's Christ"* (Luke 2:26). What convincing proof of His dual nature as God manifested in the flesh, in that He was both a *"babe...lying in a manger"* and *"Christ the Lord"*!

Yet another striking aspect of this account of the angelic visitation at the time of Christ's birth is the description of such a vast number of angels—a *"multitude of the heavenly host"* (Luke 2:13). The term *"multitude"* raises the question of how many angels actually were present at the birth of Jesus. As to their exact number, Scripture is silent, only using language implying a vast contingent of them. And these may have been but a small portion of the total number that daily inhabit heaven and earth. As Milton wrote in *Paradise Lost,*

> Nor think, though men were none,
> That heaven would want spectators, God want praise.
> Millions of spiritual creatures walk the Earth
> Unseen, both when we wake, and when we sleep:
> All these with ceaseless praise his works behold
> Both day and night.
>
> (4:675–680)

---

51. Quoted in Jamieson, *Commentary*, 99.

That angels are to be counted by the myriads throughout the illimitable universe of God is seen in the language used of them in the Bible. From the whirlwind at the end of the book of Job, the Lord spoke of them as of the multitudinous stars: *"when the morning stars sang together, and all the sons of God shouted for joy"* (Job 38:7). When Jacob returned to Paddan-aram, *"the angels of God met him"* (Genesis 32:1), and so *"he called the name of that place Mahanaim"* (Genesis 32:2), meaning two hosts or armies. The psalmist sang, *"The chariots of God are twenty thousand, even thousands of angels"* (Psalm 68:17 KJV). Similar language was used by Micaiah, who spoke of a *"host of heaven"* (1 Kings 22:19) surrounding God's throne, and by Elisha's servant, who saw the mountain *"full of horses and chariots of fire"* (2 Kings 6:17) when Elisha prayed that he might see *"those who are with us"* (verse 16). And Daniel spoke of *"a thousand thousands"* and *"ten thousand times ten thousand"* (Daniel 7:10) standing before the Ancient of Days.

In the New Testament, when Jesus prevented Peter from defending Him against His foes, He spoke of *"twelve legions of angels"* (Matthew 26:53) of all ranks as being ready to rally to His aid, if He so wished. A legion was the largest division of the Roman army, composed of 6,200 foot soldiers and 300 horse soldiers. Thus, twelve legions would represent well over 72,000. It is because of the impressive size of a legion that the term came to represent a large number in orderly combination, such as the *"myriads of myriads and thousands of thousands"* whom John heard around the throne of God in his revelation. (See Revelation 5:11.) Such numbers are symbolic of the countless throng that Milton described as "numbers without number."[52]

The ancient writer Hesiod, even though he was not an inspired author of Scripture, still acknowledged the existence of angels and wrote of their ministry to men on earth in these lines from *Works and Days*:

> Aerial spirits, by great Jove designed,
> To be on earth the guardians of mankind;
> Invisible to mortal eyes they go,
> And mark our actions, good or bad, below;
> Th' immortal spies with watchful care preside,
> And thrice ten thousand round their charges glide:
> They can reward with glory or with gold;
> A power, they by divine permission hold.

---

52. *Paradise Lost*, 3:346.

But perhaps the most striking and memorable aspect of Luke's account of the angelic visitation at the time of Jesus' birth is the *song of the angels*. This is doubtless what makes the most lasting impression on readers of the account. If those of earth, apart from the few humble folk who had received the revelation of the great mystery of godliness, were silent at the coming of the King, the skies were vocal with praise as heaven sent forth all its armies to escort the Eternal Son into our world and pay homage to Him as the One worthy of royal honors. If, as the King Himself came to declare, "*There is joy in the presence of the angels of God*" (Luke 15:10 KJV, NKJV) over the repentance of one sinner, then surely all heavenly principalities and powers must have been thrilled at the greatest event in human history, namely, the incarnation of the One who was to bring many souls to glory. If, at the creation of the world, "*the morning stars sang together, and all the sons of God shouted for joy*" (Job 38:7), how could even one seraph be silent when the world was about to receive its promised Redeemer? Why, the angelic choir sang a cradle song to the Babe born in Bethlehem such as never was sung to a monarch's son; for in those swaddling clothes was wrapped the grand mystery angels desired to look into.

How the midnight air must have vibrated as the singing of the heavenly choristers suddenly burst upon the ears of the already awestruck shepherds! Did they not listen to the greatest song ever given to earth? Never before, or since, has the world been privileged to hear a massed choir of such a vast number as this one that existed to praise God, and which had only a few poor shepherds as an audience. As "[God] *manifested in the flesh*," Jesus was "*seen by angels*," Paul said. And what a force it must have given to their singing as they beheld their Creator and Lord as a Babe wrapped in swaddling clothes! Those angelic songsters were "like an army celebrating peace," said Bengal.[53] Of their singing (in which Gabriel must have joined, seeing the heavenly host had come to seal and celebrate the good and joyful tidings he had just brought), Olshausen said they were "transferring the occupation of their exalted station to this poor earth, who so seldom resounds with the pure praise of God."[54] This "let it be known how this event is regarded in *heaven* and should be regarded on *earth*."[55]

The anthem the angels sang in notes of triumphant gladness also ascended to heaven with the melody of thanksgiving to God. The angelic song soared to heaven, then stooped to earth and concluded with men, as though it would

---

53. Quoted in Jamieson, *Commentary*, 249.
54. Ibid., 249.
55. Jamieson, *Commentary*, 249.

forever echo in human hearts—which, of course, it has. A comment from Nitzsch reminds us that at the very heart of this song, praise "rises up to the glory of God, comes down again to proffer peace to earth; rests with good-will on men....How is the glory of God manifested in the making earth peaceful, by mercy and good-will shown to sinful man"[56]!

As for the substance of the song of the celestial choir from Luke 2:14 (KJV), although it is expressed in only twelve words, it is yet of great scope. We will take, in order, its three brief, unforgettable parts.

"Glory to God in the highest." This first note gives harmony to the remaining two lines, seeing it is the assurance of what will be accomplished through the redemptive work of the One who was born as a child and given as a son. (See Isaiah 9:6.) If humans fail to grasp that, in the words of the Westminster Catechism, their "chief end is to glorify God, and to enjoy Him for ever," angels certainly made such a blessed end their main objective. Actually, in their theme song, the angels affirmed that because Jesus was born the Savior, on account of His work in saving sinners, defeating the devil, abolishing death, and making an end of sin, there should arise a new revenue of glory to God. If, in *creation*, God's omnipotence, wisdom, and love were revealed—including His judgment, with the swift vengeance that overtook the angels who sinned—then God's justice was manifested in *redemption*, when He displayed, through the coming of the Redeemer, His matchless grace—an attribute of the Godhead now fully displayed, and which the angels praised in their exaltation of divine glory.

Those holy, happy angels adored *divine wisdom* in the solution of the difficult problem of how the glory of a thrice-holy God and the salvation of guilty sinners could be harmonized—how one could be displayed as the other was maintained.

Those seraphic singers also magnified *divine holiness* as they saw the Father pass the sword of judgment into the bosom of His only begotten, well-beloved Son, just born as the Sin-Bearer.

Those celestial, joyous hosts likewise praised *divine justice*, as they discovered that the Surety must die so that sinners might live; that no general act of amnesty would pardon the guilty, but that God would punish their sins in Jesus, His Son, who died *"the righteous for the unrighteous, that he might bring us to God"* (1 Peter 3:18).

---

56. Quoted in Rudolf Stier, *The Words of the Angels* (London: Nimmo and Bain, 1879), 56.

Those "sons of the morning" also extolled *divine power*, which was to be more preeminently illustrated in the salvation of the lost than it could have been in their destruction, more abundantly illustrated in redemption than in creation.

"*On earth peace*." How true it is that there would be no real peace on earth, except it come in a way honorable to God and consistent with His divine glory. The original, blessed communion with God was forfeited by Adam through disobedience, and so the two could no longer walk together. How, then, was the breach to be healed? Certainly not by anything the estranged sinner could do, who, left to himself, must perish. The proverb has it: "Man's extremity is God's opportunity"; and God maintained His character as a God of truth and justice when His glory was revealed in human form in the Babe lying in a manger, the Babe who, on a cross, was to marry "*mercy and truth*" and enable "*righteousness and peace*" to "[kiss] *each other*" (Psalm 85:10 KJV).

Those heavenly songsters could glorify God, for the revelation thrilled their heart that their Lord, through the blood He would shed, would provide sinners with a justification by faith and consequently peace with God. Paul's prayer for the faithful in Rome was that they might have "*all joy and peace in believing*" (Romans 15:13). As for the Thessalonian church, the apostolic benediction for her members was, similarly, that "*the Lord of peace himself give you peace at all times in all ways*" (2 Thessalonians 3:16).

"*Goodwill toward men*." The Word becoming flesh and dwelling among men was the visible expression of the goodwill of God toward men. Such goodwill dates from eternity, having existed in the Divine heart long before it took human form and appeared among men. The incarnation, then, was "*according to the eternal purpose which [God] has realized in Christ Jesus our Lord*" (Ephesians 3:11). The long-looked-for redemption came according to the "*good pleasure of his will, to the praise of the glory of his grace*" (Ephesians 1:5–6 KJV). God's will toward men was *goodwill*, and it was fully revealed when the Son of the Highest bowed the heavens and, divesting Himself of His garment of light, clothed Himself in human form and inspired the angels thereby to rend the skies with their song of praise. Again, the marvel is that our humanity is the robe our Redeemer wears in heaven, and that through His grace, we have become "*partakers of the divine nature*" (2 Peter 1:4)—"*heirs of God and fellow heirs with Christ*" (Romans 8:17).

If the fruits of redemption—glory to God, peace on earth, and goodwill toward men—inspired angels' songs, should they not be the subject of higher strains and loftier raptures on the part of those who, having received Jesus as their personal Savior, strive to honor Him as Christ the Lord? As Canon Bell forcefully reminded us:

> Thus praising God we shall be in harmony with those celestial hosts, who, leaving their station before the throne of God, and speeding downwards from star to star, hovered over the stable at Bethlehem; and as they anticipated the triumphs which the Divine Babe was to win—man saved; death destroyed; the devil vanquished, and creation redeemed, gave vent to their joy in the jubilant song: "Glory to God in the highest, on earth peace, goodwill toward men."[57]

Or, as Jamieson's *Commentary* puts it, the song of the angels is a

> brief but transporting hymn—not only in articulate human speech, for our behoof, but in tunable measure, in the form of a Hebrew parallelism of two complete clauses, and a third one only amplifying the second, and so without a connecting "and." The *"glory to God,"* which the newborn "Savior" was to bring, is the first note of this sublime hymn: to this answers, in the second clause, the *"peace on earth,"* of which He was to be "the Prince" (Isaiah 9:6)—probably sung responsively by the celestial choir: while quick follows the glad echo of this note, probably by a third detachment of the angelic choristers—*"good will to men."* "They say not, glory to God in *heaven,* where the angels are, but, using a rare expression, 'in the highest [heavens],' whither angels aspire not." (Hebrews 1:3–4) "Peace" with God is the grand necessity of a fallen world. To bring in this, and all other peace in its train, was the prime errand of the Savior to this earth, and, along with it, heaven's whole "good will to men"—the Divine complacency on a new footing—descends to rest upon men, as upon the Son Himself, in whom God is "well-pleased." (Matthew 3:17, the same word as here.)[58]

We cannot meditate upon the carol sung by angels on that first Christmas Day without thinking of the tragic contrast between that carol introducing the Christian faith and the fearful condition of the world today after 2,000 years of

---

57. Charles Dent Bell, *Angelic Beings: Their Nature and Ministry* (London: Religious Tract Society, 1875), 70.
58. Jamieson, *Commentary*, 249–250. The quotation within the passage is from Bengal.

Christianity. What a God-rejecting age, rather than a God-glorifying one, we live in! Among the teeming millions of earth, very few have any desire to re-echo the first line of the angels' song. Even in so-called Christian nations, there is a practical atheism found in the pagan idea that lives on the practical assumption that if there is a God, He is far removed from our human life; that one may live without reference to Him for the needs of life; that, actually, He is not required. Such pagan secularism contends that Christianity, with its preeminent basic concept of glorifying God in the highest, is one for monks and nuns to adopt in their monastic lives.

The angels who sang the message from heaven of goodwill toward men must sob as they look down on human society and see how it is now characterized by ill will toward men. Cheerfully, the angels thought of humanity becoming one holy, happy family; but it must make them weep as they realize that men, in their sin, do not think alike cheerfully of themselves and others. Goodwill is a very scarce commodity in human relations today. Violence, hooliganism, robbery, kidnapping, deceit, jealousy, suspicion, and killings are widespread in so-called civilized countries. Even among professing Christians, goodwill is a virtue that is not practiced as it should be. As Robert Burns said, "Man's inhumanity to man makes countless thousands mourn!"—both angels and men.

As for "peace on earth," what a misnomer this line in the joyful songsters' birthday hymn has been. That musical word—*peace*—is a promise full of victory; but ever since it was sung by the angelic choristers, the history of the world has been written in blood. Our earth today is distracted by wars and rumors of wars that are bred in the wild passions and unsanctified lusts and ambitions of men. All nations are arming themselves to the teeth because of fear of each other. *Peace!* Why, even the church is like *"a house divided against itself"* (Matthew 12:25), full of the din of controversy and strife, torn asunder by factional divisions and unseemly contentions.

But, blessed be God, we are assured that swords will yet be beaten into plowshares and spears into pruning hooks. (See Isaiah 2:4.) While the vision of a peaceful world tarries, the angels' song yet echoes in every land, *"for the earth will be filled with the knowledge of the glory of the Lord, as the waters cover the sea"* (Habakkuk 2:14). When the Prince of Peace appears, a restored and regenerated earth will raise the seraphic anthem to heaven: *"Glory to God in the highest, and on earth peace, goodwill toward men!"* (Luke 2:14 NKJV).

ANGELS AT JESUS' TEMPTATION

Let us now consider the message and the ministry of angels at the time of the temptation of Jesus. It is to be regretted that the doings and sayings of these wonderful, ministering spirits have not claimed the reverent attention they should have. The fascinating subject of angelic ministrations has fallen out of notice to a degree that is admittedly strange, considering how Jesus Himself was ministered to by angels and how frequently He referred to the sending of angels in order that His Father's purposes might be fulfilled. Did He not represent these celestial hosts as eternal, sympathizing witnesses of all that occurs in heaven and in earth? Are they not charged by God to keep the saints in all their way, and have they not a glory all their own? When Jesus, as the Son of Man, comes in judgment, it will be *"in his glory and the glory of the Father and of the holy angels"* (Luke 9:26).

In our discussion of the temptation of Jesus in chapter 2, we touched upon the comforting, strengthening aid He received after the contest with the devil. All through His experience in the wilderness, Jesus had no recourse to His deity or to angels for help and relief. But, as Jamieson wrote, "After having refused to claim the *illegitimate* ministration of angels in His behalf, oh, with what deep joy would He accept their services when sent, unasked, at the close of all this Temptation, direct from Him Whom He had so gloriously honored?"[59] As soon as His exhausting encounter with the apostate angel was over, He gladly welcomed the beneficial ministration of the army of heaven. *"Behold, angels came and ministered to him"* (Matthew 4:11). The only matter we seek to raise once more in this section is what kind of angelic service it was that Jesus received once the defeated devil had left Him.

Witnessing Him whom they had known, loved, worshipped, and obeyed since His creation of them, the holy angels must have been deeply moved as they beheld Jesus as the Man, weak and hungry because of His long fast, enduring such temptation, without asking them to aid Him in His trial. We can rest assured, however, that those heavenly helpers mutually planned how they would assist Him in His worn-out condition once the devil had left Him. Their heartfelt and direct purpose was to bring Jesus necessary supplies for the refreshment of His weak and wearied humanity. Again, with what exact provisions they ministered to Him we are not particularly informed. The original words appear to suggest the spreading of a table for Him by the angels in the presence of His enemies.

---

59. Jamieson, *Commentary*, 26.

(See Psalm 23:5.) The term translated *"ministered"* in Matthew 4:11 is used in connection with the supply of material sustenance in Mark 1:31, which describes how Simon's mother-in-law *"served"* Jesus and four of His disciples; and it is used in Luke 8:3, which describes how several women traveled with Jesus and His disciples and *"provided for them out of their means."*

Elijah of old, when hungry, was furnished with food by an angel who evidently was able to make exceedingly good nourishing cakes, enabling the prophet to continue his journey to *"the mount of God"* (1 Kings 19:6–8). Whatever the nature of *"angels' food"* (Psalm 78:25 KJV, NKJV), it was a repast that relieved and refreshed the Lord of angels; and as He partook of it, He doubtless heard a voice from heaven saying, once again, "This is My beloved Son, in whom I am well pleased." But do we really grasp that ours is a greater privilege in our temptations? After His conquest of the tempter, Jesus had angels to aid, dress, and look after Him; but in and after our encounters with the devil and evil forces, we have Jesus Himself to rally to our help and need. As we emerge victorious from a wrestle with satanic principalities and powers, heaven smiles, succors, and sustains the faithful heart; and the stress and strain of trial are more than repaired by the gracious, willing ministries of Him who is ever at hand to undertake.

Is this not the truth taught us in that great Scripture in the book of Hebrews, *"For because he himself has suffered and been tempted, he is able to help those who are tempted"* (Hebrews 2:18)? The Greek word translated here as *"help"* implies to run to answer a cry for help, or to advance in aid of someone. It occurs in only one other place in the New Testament, 2 Corinthians 6:2: *"At the acceptable time I have listened to you, and helped you on the day of salvation."* Jesus was *"made like his brethren in every respect"* (Hebrews 2:17), and because He has been tempted, He now has the special ability and willingness to come to the aid of those who are tempted, because of His sympathy and His knowledge of the help needed, as well as by His position of High Priest, which He gained through suffering. Having been tempted in all points as we are, He is able to help us, in an even more perfect way than angels, in all possible trials and temptations common to man. (See Hebrews 4:15.)[60] As Jamieson's *Commentary* notes in regard to these passages, "Not only as God He knows our trials, but also as man He knows them by experimental feeling."[61] His holy example during temptation exhibited the way in which we, too, can be victorious, namely, by the skillful use of Scripture, suffering according to

60. Jamieson, *Commentary*, 446.
61. Ibid.

the will of God, assured that by His mighty Spirit and by the beneficial visitations and ministrations of His angels, we will receive aid and deliverance from Him. In the words of Benjamin Beddome's hymn "If Christ Is Mine":

> If He is mine, I need not fear
> The rage of earth and hell;
> He will support my feeble frame,
> And all their power repel.

ANGELS AND JESUS' PUBLIC TEACHING

The angels witnessed and revealed the purposes God was accomplishing through Jesus during the days of His flesh. At the same time, in His public teaching, He had much to say about their nature and ministry. Much as we would like to linger over an exposition of this subject, it is not strictly within the province of our topic, that is, how Jesus was *"seen by angels,"* as expressed in the creedal chant we are considering. But, for the guidance of those who desire to pursue such a profitable theme, we herewith append Hastings' outline on these intermediaries between God and man:

+ Their dwelling place is in heaven (Matthew 18:[10]; Luke [2:13,1 15]; John 1:51).

+ They are superior to men, but in the world to come, the righteous will have equality with them (Luke 20:34–36).

+ They carry away the souls of the righteous to a place of rest (Luke 16:22).

+ They are (as seems to be suggested) of neither sex (Matthew 22:30).

+ They are very numerous (Matthew 26:53).

+ They will appear with Christ at His second advent. Most of His references to angels are associated with this truth (Matthew 13:39; 16:27; 24:31; 25:31; Mark 8:38; Luke 9:26).

+ There are bad as well as good angels (Matthew 25:41). It is usually to the latter that reference is made.

+ They are limited in knowledge (Matthew 24:36).

+ There are guardian angels of children (Matthew 18:10).

+ They rejoice at the triumph of good (Luke 15:10).

ANGELS AND JESUS' SUFFERINGS

Jesus was *"seen by angels"* not only at His birth and after His temptation but also during the time of His sufferings. These sufferings began with Christ's agony in the garden. While all four Gospels describe this event, it is Luke who adds three particulars unmentioned by the other three: *"There appeared unto him an angel from heaven, strengthening him"*; *"being in an agony he prayed more earnestly"*; and *"his sweat became as it were great drops of blood falling down upon the ground"* (Luke 22:43–44 RV). We do not know if the multitude of angels who witnessed and welcomed His birth, or the company selected to minister to His needs after His temptation, were beholders of His agony in the garden of Gethsemane. If they were, then they must have been moved with deep pity for their suffering Lord. Being capable of joy, the angels are also capable of grief; and much grief must have been theirs as they witnessed His bloody sweat accompanied by *"loud cries and tears"* (Hebrews 5:7). As Benjamin Beddome wrote in his hymn "Did Christ O'er Sinners Weep?":

> The Son of God in tears
> The wondering angels see:
> Be thou astonished, O my soul;
> He shed those tears for thee.

The extreme anguish that Jesus experienced occasioned the visitation of a specially designated angel from heaven. So one was sent, probably Gabriel, who is depicted as standing in God's presence awaiting His call. (See Luke 1:19.) He it was who announced the birth of Jesus and who may have appeared to indicate that all heavenly intelligences were with Jesus in the battles of heaven against sin and hell. But, before dealing with the exact way this privileged angel consoled and strengthened Jesus, a brief reference must be made to the solemn circumstances necessitating the ministration of this heavenly visitant.

In a most vehement way, Jesus expressed His anguish of soul through His heartrending cry, *"My soul is very sorrowful, even to death"* (Matthew 26:38). *"Even to death"*!—not the preordained, predicted death of the cross, but the fear that He might die before that final triumph at Calvary. *"Greatly distressed and troubled"* (Mark 4:33), heavily oppressed, and crushed with sorrow over the events of previous days that culminated in His tragic betrayal by Judas—one of the Twelve whom He had chosen—Jesus, in the anguish of His heart, said, in effect, "I feel as if nature would sink under this load, as if life were ebbing out, and death coming before its time."[62]

Timpson reminded us that many commentators of a past century suggested that in this extreme suffering of our Lord, He struggled with legions of the spirits of darkness, surrounded by a mighty host of devils who exercised all their force and malice to persecute and distract His innocent soul. According to these commentators, Satan hoped that by overpowering Jesus with his agents in Gethsemane, he could prevent the fulfillment of the divine prophecies relating to the manner of the Redeemer's death, and so defeat the design of our redemption.

Elsewhere, we have drawn attention to the efforts of the devil, who had the power of death, to kill Jesus before He reached the cross to die by crucifixion—as both psalmist and prophet portrayed long before such a cruel mode of death for criminals was invented by the Romans. Do the phrases *"very sorrowful, even to death,"* *"being in an agony,"* and *"sweat became as it were great drops of blood"* indicate that Gethsemane was the devil's last attempt to end the life of Jesus before the surrender of that life to death on the cross? Was this part of the mixture of the cup that Jesus prayed might pass from Him, seeing He had declared that no man—or devil, for that matter—was able to take His life from Him? (See John 10:18.) Since redemption could be purchased only at the costly price that Paul called *"the blood of [God's] own Son"* (Acts 20:28), then the death He was born to die was one that none could nullify.

It is significant that as Jesus reached Gethsemane, He said to His disciples, *"Watch and pray that you may not enter into temptation"* (Matthew 26:41)—a temptation He Himself was about to face. Temptation presupposes forces and figures that tempt. The plea of Jesus was thus an echo of the prayer He taught His disciples to pray: *"Lead us not into temptation, but deliver us from evil"* (Matthew 6:13)—the evil lurking in the temptation. The disciples now saw the clause used in all the fullness of its meaning, as Jesus entered a season of trial and suffering from which He would not shrink. Humanlike, Jesus felt the need of company to console Him in His hour of conflict, and so requested of His followers, *"Remain here, and watch with me"* (Matthew 26:38). But they failed Him, preferring sleep to a vigilant watch. They slept as He suffered. Not so the alert angel who came to His aid, and this time not *after* His season of spiritual, bodily, and mental exertion but *during* it. Gabriel (if that is who it was), along with his God and our God and all the angels, *"will neither slumber nor sleep"* (Psalm 121:4).

---

62. Jamieson, *Commentary*, 343.

The wonder is that even as Jesus bore "a weight of woe more than ten worlds could bear,"[63] He did not draw upon His reserve of deity to strengthen and sustain Him in that grim experience but accepted the assistance of an angel. Being made *"lower than the angels"* (Hebrews 2:9) in His humiliation, He was capable of receiving help from one of them.[64] Thus, as the surges rose higher, beating more tempestuously until it seemed as if they would overcome Him, in the bitterness of His feared death, the angel appeared to fortify Him, to brace up His sinking form. "He has anticipated and rehearsed His final conflict and won the victory— now on the theatre of an *invincible will,* as then on the arena of the cross. 'I will suffer,' is the grand result of Gethsemane: 'It is finished' is the shout that bursts from the cross."[65]

While the disciples proved themselves to be miserable comforters and broken reeds, the solicitous seraph *strengthened* Him, Luke tells us. Although several commentators have made conjectures as to the form or nature of the strength imparted, Luke does not give us any particulars as to the angelic messenger's ministry of love to the suffering Redeemer. The English word *strengthen* can be translated from a variety of Greek terms. Shortly before entering the garden of Gethsemane, for example, Jesus urged His disciples to *"strengthen"* one another (see Luke 22:32); that word means "to fix firmly," "to make steadfast." But the word for how the angel strengthened Jesus is different and implies "to in-strengthen, invigorate, make strong." For the assistance of Jesus against the powers of darkness, the angel from heaven, evidently in a visible form, stood by Him and invigorated Him by being a tangible sign of the Father's protection and favor and by suggesting such holy consolations as were calculated to animate His soul in such a struggle.

Matthew Henry suggested this about the angel's aid:

Perhaps he...wiped away his sweat and tears, perhaps ministered some cordial to him, as after his temptation, or, it may be, took him by the arm, and helped him off the ground, or bore him up when he was ready to faint away; and in these services of the angel, the holy Spirit was... putting strength into him: for so the word signifies.[66]

---

63. Quoted in James Hervey, *Theron and Aspasio* (London: Thomas Tegg, 1837), 62.
64. Matthew Henry, *An Exposition of the Old and New Testament* (New York: Carter and Brothers, 1856), 4:541.
65. Jamieson, *Commentary,* 151.
66. Henry, *Exposition of the Old and New Testament,* 4:541.

Whatever comforts the angel ministered to relieve Jesus in His human anguish, Jesus was pleased to receive such from one of His own creation, just as God receives glory from His creatures. That the angelic aid was beneficial is seen in the way Jesus responded after He had been raised up from the cold ground, had His fainting head supported, and had the bloody sweat washed from His deathlike face: *"Rise; let us be going"* (Matthew 26:46). Jesus appeared fresh and glorious in His visage, as if filled with renewed courage after having defeated a savage foe. Such was the effort of the angel's ministry that those who came to apprehend Jesus as He emerged from the garden fell backward to the ground as He presented Himself and simply said, *"I am he"* (John 18:6). Thus Matthew Henry commented that in the garden, "Christ entered the list with the powers of darkness, gave them all advantages, and yet conquered."[67]

The lesson we learn from the interposition of the angel as he saw and strengthened Jesus is that when human comforters fail, as His disciples left Him alone—when our nearest friends fail in ability to render us needful aid—heavenly ministering forces are at hand to succor and comfort. God Himself, as the *"God of all comfort"* (2 Corinthians 1:3), will be the strength of our hearts and our portion forever. (See Psalm 73:26.) And this was at least one episode during the sufferings of Jesus when He was *"seen by angels,"* who witnessed and, by their presence, bore testimony to His struggles as He became the Redeemer of mankind.

Scripture is silent as to whether, when Jesus was dying—in the eyes of a godless world, as a felon on a wooden gibbet—He was seen by angels. We have no record of an angel appearing for His rescue or relief when, as the Man of Sorrows, He carried the load of the world's guilt and when, as He was *"stricken, smitten by God, and afflicted"* (Isaiah 53:4), He made reconciliation for iniquity. Yet because there is joy in the presence of the celestial spirits over one sinner repenting, there must have been praise among them as they received the news of the salvation of His fellow sufferer, the dying thief, who rejoiced to see the fountain for sin and uncleanness opened in his day. This repentant thief was the first fruit of Christ's death as the sinless Substitute for sinners.

ANGELS AND JESUS' RESURRECTION

But once Jesus, whom death could not hold (see Acts 2:24), *rose from the dead,* the angels were at the tomb, not to only guard His lifeless body while it reposed

---

67. Matthew Henry, *The Holy Bible…and a Commentary* (London: Religious Tract Society, 1835), 308.

therein but also to announce His resurrection to life, even as they had celebrated His entrance into our life at birth. The angels who witnessed the resurrection included the angel who rolled away the stone of the tomb and announced the event to the women who had arrived early at the place of burial (see Matthew 28:1–7), the two angels who guarded the tomb and introduced the risen Lord to Mary Magdalene (see John 20:11–14), and those in the *"vision of angels"* (Luke 24:23) that testified to these women about what took place at the resurrection. Let us consider how they witnessed to the purposes of God in this supreme event in the life of Jesus.

As a dramatic introduction to the most outstanding miracle of history, God caused a supernatural earthquake in Jerusalem (see Matthew 28:2), which shook the entire city and caused the inhabitants to reflect upon their crime of having *"crucified the Lord of glory"* (1 Corinthians 2:8). This earthquake likewise prepared the way for the angelic announcement of His victorious triumph over the grave and Satan. Such a convulsion must have also struck terror into the hearts of the Roman guards, as the rocking earth made them tremble and become *"like dead men"* (Matthew 28:4). In their consternation, they sought to ascertain the mysterious cause of the earth tremor and were immediately arrested by the visible presence of a heavenly being who had been sent by the omnipotent God as His official from the court of His palace.

Those Imperial guards, and all the formidable weapons of the Roman army, were no match for an angel armed with the might of God. Vainly did the soldiers defend the sacred tomb of Jesus, for that one angel was well able to roll away the very great stone sealing its entrance, which was intended to prevent any attempt to steal the nail-scarred body. (See Matthew 27:62–66.) Military array and destructive weapons employed to defend the burial place were useless against the strength of the angel, who removed the stone and *"sat upon it"* (Matthew 28:2). What ignominy that must have been to proud Rome, to see an angel making a seat of the stone, sitting at ease, in defiance of the mightiest legions of the then-mistress of the world! Seated with perfect composure, as a servant in waiting, the angel, in effect, was saying to the armed guards, "You may retire from your present charge and report what has now transpired, for I design to remain here on guard, to wait upon Jesus, who was crucified, and to fulfill the orders of my injured Master."

This fearless guardian angel is described by Mark as *"a young man"* (Mark 16:5). Matthew says that his *"appearance was like lightning, and his raiment white as snow"* (Matthew 28:3). "Lightning dressed like snow" is reckoned to be the finest expression that human language can furnish to describe the appearance of an inhabitant of heaven. How dull, then, must the splendor of this world appear, and how mean its finest dress, before the brilliant luster of an angel clothed in a spotless robe! How glorious and terrible to guilty mortals must be the appearance of angels! Good men like Daniel, Manoah, and other holy persons have been overwhelmed by their splendor and unable to bear the sight of them without trembling. (See Daniel 8:17; Judges 13:22.)

The two words that stand out in the description of this dazzling angel are *"appearance"* and *"raiment,"* the former expressing the *glory* and the latter the *purity* of the glorious and holy abode from which he came. The prostrate condition of those dreaded Roman warriors indicates what effect the brilliant angel had on them. In the words of the psalmist: *"The stouthearted were stripped of their spoil; they sank into sleep; all the men of war were unable to use their hands"* (Psalm 76:5).

Mary, who had come to the tomb, feared that some strange thing may have happened to the body of her precious Lord, and so she *"stood weeping outside the tomb, and as she wept she stooped to look into the tomb; and she saw two angels in white, sitting where the body of Jesus had lain, one at the head and one at the feet"* (John 20:11–12). These angelic guardians had been watching the body that had housed God manifested in the flesh. Note the words *"had lain":* He was not there anymore, as Mary came to learn when she met her risen Master alive forevermore. Is it not moving to observe that the first words of Jesus after His glorious victory were directed to a woman who was still devoting herself to a love that had all along been shown toward Him, and that when Mary fully recognized Him, she cried excitedly, *"Rabboni!"* (John 20:16)? "She had heard in the well-known voice her own name, and it…brought back to her all the old associations."[68]

What stupendous news the dazzling angelic herald flashed to heaven and earth, and even to hell: *"He is not here: for he has risen, as he said"* (Matthew 28:6)! Each phrase in this angelic proclamation is rich in meaning and announces what God has done through Jesus.

"He is not here" is the message of the *empty tomb.* It is most beneficial for us that He was not there, for, had the grave continued to possess His dead body, we would have been of all men most to be pitied (see 1 Corinthians 15:19), having no salvation, no hope of eternal life. Paul told us that if Jesus had remained in

68. Charles John Ellicott, *A New Testament Commentary for English Readers* (London: Cassell, Petter, Galpin & Co., 1884), I:542.

the tomb, then preaching and faith would be in vain. (See 1 Corinthians 15:14.) What a charming invitation the angel gave to the women who had come to pay their respects to the dead: *"Come, see the place where he lay"* (Matthew 28:6). But He was no longer in the place where they had helped to lay Him; and how amazed they must have been to hear the assuring angel say, in essence, "Come see the place where the Lord of glory lay; now it is an empty grave. He lies not there, though He once lay there. Come, feast your eyes upon it!"

Had death kept its prey another day, corruption that ordinarily ensues would have set in. Martha, sister of dead Lazarus, said to Jesus when He visited the grave at Bethany, *"Lord, by this time there will be an odor, for he has been dead four days"* (John 11:39)—the offensive smell being proof that decomposition had set in. But the prophecy regarding Jesus was that God would not suffer His Holy One to remain to see corruption (see Psalm 16:10 KJV, NKJV), so He was raised from the dead on the third day and thus saw no corruption.

It is impossible to fix the exact moment when Jesus burst the bars of death and rose triumphant, but the indications are that it was about sunrise. *"Mary Magdalene and the other Mary"* came to the sepulcher *"toward the dawn"* (Matthew 28:1). Ellicott remarked that "there was an obvious fitness in the symbolism of the Resurrection of the Son of Righteousness coinciding with the natural 'day-spring.'"[69]

"He has risen" is the message of *eternal triumph.* The empty tomb and the angel's positive declaration testify to the most glorious fact of our Christian faith. On the Lord's Day, and on every day, we should praise the Lord for His eternal victory over sin, death, and the devil and rejoice in such a birthday of all our hopes. As that eminent divine poet, Doddridge, expressed it:

> Now is the justice of God amply satisfied, or the prisoner had never been released. Now is the reproach of the cross ceased, and turned into proportionable glory. That reproach was rolled away at once by the descending angel, who appeared, not to awaken Christ from His sleep, or bring Him a new life...but he came to add a solemn pomp to His revival, and to strike the guards with such a terror as would effectually prevent any mad attempt on this glorious Conqueror when he was bursting the bonds in which he had for a while been held.[70]

---

69. Charles John Ellicott, ed., *The New Testament Commentary for Schools: The Gospel According to St. Mark* (London: Cassell, Petter, Galpin & Co., 1879), 263.
70. Philip Doddridge, *The Family Expositor* (London: Westley and Davis, 1831), 348.

Now is Christ indeed *"risen from the dead, and become the firstfruits of them that slept"* (1 Corinthians 15:20 KJV). No wonder Paul concluded his marvelous exposition on the resurrection of Christ with this glorious crescendo:

> *"Death is swallowed up in victory." O death, where is thy victory? O death, where is thy sting?*   (1 Corinthians 15:54–55)

In his hymn "Yes, the Redeemer Rose," Doddridge summarized in poetic form the witness and ministry of the angels in connection with the resurrection:

> Lo! The angelic bands
> In full assembly meet,
> To wait His high commands,
> And worship at His feet:
> Joyful they come,
> And wing their way,
> From realms of day,
> To Jesus' tomb.
> Then back to heav'n they fly
> And the glad tidings bear.
> Hark! As they soar on high,
> What music fills the air!
> Their anthems say,
> "Jesus, who bled,
> Hath left the dead;
> He rose today."

Finally, *"as he said"* is the message of *established truth*. Rising again from the dead, Jesus verified or established the veracity of ancient predictions, as well as His own, to His everlasting conquest of death. *"As he said"*! What had He said regarding His ignominious death and glorious resurrection? Listen to His masterly challenge, what He said about His own life: *"I have power to lay it down, and I have power to take it again"* (John 10:18). "I have power to lay down My life." At Calvary, this is what He did, for His death was voluntary. His life was not taken but *given*. He did not die as a victim but as the Victor. *"I have power to take it again,"* meaning that He rose again by His own volition as the Son of God with power.

Since Jesus said that the Holy Spirit was the source of His power during His ministry as a Man among men—*"If it is by the Spirit of God that I cast out demons,*

then the kingdom of God has come upon you" (Matthew 12:28)—it is interesting
to know that the Comforter was also active with Jesus in His resurrection. Paul
spoke of *"the Spirit of him who raised Jesus from the dead"* (Romans 8:11). Again,
Rome had placed the imperial seal on the heavy stone outside the tomb, where
her mighty warriors stood guard to see that Jesus did not leave; but God had His
seal inside, assuring that His Son would rise again. Is not the Holy Spirit the
divine Seal? (See Ephesians 1:13.) In this manner God raised up Jesus from the
dead. (See, for example, Romans 8:11; Acts 2:24.)

We have so far spoken of the angel who rolled away the stone, and of the two
angels who guarded the tomb, but we have not yet spoken of the *"vision of angels"*
(Luke 24:23) that Luke tells us the women who came early to the sepulcher later
testified to having seen. Unfortunately, the Scriptures give us no further details
of this vision, except that the angels in it *"said that he was alive."* In this case, as
well, the angels were instruments of God's revelation, announcing how His purposes were being fulfilled in all the events of Jesus' life.

The important aspect of our meditation on the meaning of Jesus' resurrection was expressed by Paul in the words, "...*as Christ was raised from the dead by
the glory of the Father, we too might walk in newness of life*" (Romans 6:4). If we thus
share His risen life, then *"he who raised Christ Jesus from the dead will give life to
[our] mortal bodies also through his Spirit which dwells in [us]"* (Romans 8:11). The
pertinent question that the angel asked of the women as they came with their
spices to anoint the slain body of the Lord has a practical application for all who
claim to be risen with Christ: *"Why do you seek the living among the dead?"* (Luke
24:5). (In the days of His flesh, Jesus uttered a like parallel in Matthew 8:22 in
the command, *"Leave the dead to bury their own dead."*) For the sorrowing women
who came to the tomb, such a question was enough to change the whole cur-
rent of their thoughts. The Lord, whom they came to honor as dead, was indeed
"living," and as Jesus Himself says from glory, *"I am...the living one; I died, and
behold I am alive for evermore"* (Revelation 1:17–18). He who was dead, but now
is alive forevermore, does not expect to find those who are partakers of His resurrection among the dead things of the world, or in dead works. If we are risen
with Him, then we must seek the things that are above and not be found among
the worldly ambitions and amusements of a world that is dead in sin. Worldly-
minded Christians need to be reminded of what it truly means to be risen with
Him who left the place of the dead behind Him.

ANGELS AND JESUS' ASCENSION

Witnessing the glorious ascension of Jesus was the climax of the beatific vision of the angels. The solemn parting from His disciples on earth was seen by angels. Peter reminded us that the glory that would follow the sufferings of Christ was a messianic theme that the angels longed to look into. (See 1 Peter 1:11–12.) How their minds, then, would be fully satisfied with the revelation of this mystery of godliness, as they not only gazed upon their ascending Lord but also accompanied Him on His return to the glory that He had with the Father before the world began! (See John 17:5.) The ascension was a wonderful confirmation of the incarnation.

While Luke definitely states that there were two angels with assumed human form covered with white apparel attending our Lord's ascent (see Acts 1:10–11), the question is whether there were other angelic companions on that triumphal return to the Father's home. As He rose from earth, by His own divine power, in a manner worthy of His majesty as the Lord of glory who had been God manifested in the flesh, a bright cloud interposed, causing the awestruck disciples to lose sight of their beloved Master. (See Acts 1:9.) Such a brilliant cloud not only signified the splendor of His glorious body but may also represent a heaven-sent guard of angels, seeing that the appearance of angels is sometimes described as like a cloud: the Lord of angels said that He would appear in the cloud upon the mercy seat, where sat the two cherubim (see Leviticus 16:2); Daniel envisioned *"one like a son of man"* coming with *"the clouds of heaven"* (Daniel 7:13); this One came to the Ancient of Days, who was surrounded by *"a thousand thousands"* and *"ten thousand times ten thousand"* (Daniel 7:10) of the angelic host.

This cloud *"took [Jesus] out of their sight"* (Acts 1:9). One loves to feel that what actually happened was that a host of angels bore Him up as in a conqueror's chair to realms above, there to be welcomed by ten thousand times ten thousand more angelic voices singing in adoration and worship, *"Worthy is the Lamb who was slain, to receive power and wealth and wisdom and might and honor and glory and blessing!"* (Revelation 5:12). David wrote, *"The chariots of God are twenty thousand, even thousands of angels"* (Psalm 68:17–18 KJV). James Fanch wrote of the angels in his hymn "Beyond the Glittering, Starry Skies":

> They brought His chariot from above,
> To bear Him to His throne,
> Clapped their triumphant wings and cried,
> "The glorious work is done!"

When it came to the prophet Elijah's dramatic ascension, he did not rise in elegant, easy fashion, as Jesus did, but was snatched away in a whirlwind, in a chariot of fire, with fiery horses (see 2 Kings 2:11)—a departure suited to that stern reprover of an apostate race.

Further, those angels knew that the glory given to Christ at His ascension—a glory that flowed from the cross—was conferred on Him not in His divine nature (for, as God, He could not be further exalted), but because of His mediatorial work as *"the man Christ Jesus"* (1 Timothy 2:5). The angelic investigation of the sufferings of Christ that Peter mentioned included the love of God, as revealed at Calvary, for a lost world. The angels knew that *"God is love"* (1 John 4:8, 16), as their own creation and happiness proved; but for Him to love sinful man, and to surrender His Son for the propitiation of our sins, caused them to marvel. The immeasurable love of Christ, passing all knowledge, a love manifested nowhere else in such unspeakable greatness and sacrifice, was certainly one aspect of the divine nature that the angels worthily desired to look into. Jesus had been made *"a little lower than the angels for the suffering of death"* but was now *"crowned with glory and honor"* (Hebrews 2:9 KJV).

Jesus left His disciples—His church's representation, and embryo—on earth, but He was not to be detached from them. While the angels joyfully and adoringly welcomed His public entry into the Jerusalem above, He Himself revealed that He had at heart the concerns of His church to be established, and so He sent two angels in white apparel to assure His disciples that although He had been taken out of their midst, they would see Him return in the same manner as He went to heaven. While He was with them, had He not promised that they would share His heavenly abode? *"I will come again and will take you to myself, that where I am you may be also"* (John 14:3). How, then, must the faith of the men of Galilee have been confirmed and their hearts comforted to hear the twin angels announce, *"This Jesus...will come in the same way as you saw him go into heaven"* (Acts 1:11)? He who had just left them would be the very same One to return, a prophetic revelation Paul elaborated on when he wrote that *"the Lord himself will descend from heaven"* (1 Thessalonians 4:16). Then the apostle went on to record that at the rapture of the true church, angels will again be the attendants for the descending Lord, for their musical shout will be heard, and the silvery voice of the archangel (possibly Gabriel, who proclaimed Christ's first advent) will publish His second advent: *"For the Lord himself will descend from heaven with a cry of command, with the archangel's call, and with the sound of the trumpet of God"* (1 Thessalonians 4:16). So, when the redeemed *"meet the Lord in the air"* (verse 17) on their ascension to glory, they, too, will be seen by angels.

ANGELIC WORSHIP OF JESUS

As we conclude our meditation on how Jesus was *"seen by angels,"* it is intriguing to ask what was the precise occasion when the angelic host came to understand the full significance of their Creator's incarnation. In His parable of the fig tree, Jesus affirmed that at the time He spoke, angels, like men below, did not know the day or the hour of His coming judgment upon the godless earth. (See Matthew 24:36.) Being angels, they were present before time began when one of their leaders in the angelic hierarchy, Lucifer, yielding to pride and ambition, sought to be exalted as a member of the Godhead and was expelled from heaven along with those angels who rebelled with him. The remaining obedient angels doubtless heard the first pronouncement of the coming of the Son of God to earth to destroy the works of the devil and his angels, and they were gratified to know that the seed of the woman would bruise the serpent's head. (See Genesis 3:15.) A knowledge, then, was theirs of Satan's expulsion from the courts above, and of the plan of redemption, which was to involve the death of God's beloved Son.

Living in the light of the divine throne, they gathered knowledge from the fountainhead, and so learned all about God's holiness in the expulsion of their fallen companions from heaven and of the terrible judgment the devil with his angels would ultimately suffer as the result of Jesus coming in the fullness of time, as One born of a woman. The secret, however, that these inquiring angels sought to probe was how and when His incarnation would be accomplished. As the wisdom of God was bound up with the means He was to employ for the Word to be made flesh, the exact method and moment of such a transformation was one of the things those holy angels wanted a deeper insight into.

It may have been by the announcements of Gabriel to Zechariah and to Mary that the inquiring angels understood how, when, and where the promised Messiah was to be born. The broad truth that their Creator was to become a Child had been known to them from the fall of Satan and God's promise of a Deliverer, but how this miracle was to happen was the mystery solved for them when their Leader declared that He would be conceived by the Holy Spirit and born of the Virgin Mary. What rapture must have been theirs when they beheld the union of deity and humanity in a tiny Babe!

But, even though those angels desired to look into the sufferings of Christ and the glory that would follow, they knew that they would have no share in the same—that Jesus was to die on behalf of humanity, not on their behalf—they could never experience *"the fellowship of his sufferings"* and know *"the power of his resurrection"* (Philippians 3:10 KJV). Yet, although such participation can never be theirs, these heaven-sent messengers ever rejoice over all Jesus accomplished for the vindication of God's holiness and for the deliverance of sinners from the tyranny of sin. When Isaiah came to record his sublime vision, he said that he beheld how the angels veiled their faces in adoring worship of Him who was their Creator, and he heard them cry one to another, *"Holy, holy, holy is the LORD of hosts"* (Isaiah 6:3). But when John came to reveal the angelic worship of Jesus after His return as the Lamb who had taken away the sin of the world, he spoke of the uncountable number of angels whose worship and praise knew no bounds as they dwelt on their dominant theme: *"Worthy is the Lamb who was slain"* (Revelation 5:12). Those joyful angels realized that, as the result of the Word becoming flesh, dwelling among men, and ultimately dying for their redemption, He was *"much superior"* to them, and that, through His life and sacrifice, He had obtained a name *"more excellent than theirs"* (Hebrews 1:4).

The question for our hearts is that if the angels' delight in and worship of Jesus are so intense, even though they are not the beneficiaries of His redemptive work but rather the heralds of it, seeing that we owe Jesus more than angels do, should not our adoration equal or exceed that of these ministers of His will? Are we not bound to Him by ties of which they know nothing? It was not for them that He endured agony and bloody sweat and died upon the cross. Further, it is our nature, and not the nature of angels, that Jesus wears forever in heaven. Therefore, our love for Him ought to be stronger, our reverence for Him deeper, and our devotion to Him more perfect. Because He bought us at a price at which angels were not purchased, should He not find us lost in adoration, praise, and worship?

We know of no better way to conclude our meditation on this fourth line of the triumphant hymn of the early church than to quote, at full length, Fanch's impressive poem:

> Beyond the glittering starry skies,
> Far as th'eternal hills,
> There, in those boundless worlds of light,
> Our great Redeemer dwells.

Legions of angels strong and fair,
In countless armies shine,
At His right hand with golden harps,
To offer songs divine.

"Hail, Prince!" they cry, "for ever hail!
Whose unexampled love
Moved Thee to quit those glorious realms,
And royalties above."

While He did condescend on earth
To suffer rude disdain,
They cast their honors at His feet,
And waited in His train.

Through all His travels here below
They did His steps attend!
Oft gazed and wondered where at last
This scene of love would end.

They saw His heart transfixed with wounds,
His crimson sweat and gore,
They saw Him break the bars of death,
Which none e'er brake before.

They brought His chariot from above,
To bear Him to His throne,
Clapped their triumphant wings and cried,
"The glorious work is done!"

5

THE PILLAR OF PROCLAMATION

"Preached among the nations...."
—1 Timothy 3:16

The next line in the ancient "confession-chant" we are considering is, "[God] *was...preached among the nations.*" Such a statement raises several important questions. Who are these *"nations"*? Who preached to them? And what was the message that was preached? Let us take each of these questions in order.

WHO ARE THE *"NATIONS"*?

First, in Scripture, *"nations"* is a term equivalent to "Gentiles," "heathen," "peoples," "Greeks," or "strangers." All these words describe anyone who is not of the nation of Israel. The Israelites became subject to Gentile domination, and were no more under their own rulers in their own land, starting around 600 B.C., when Nebuchadnezzar, king of the mighty Babylonian Empire, subdued Jerusalem through the force of arms. The Israelites remained under Gentile domination for the rest of the period covered by the Bible, and so Gentiles figure largely in the New Testament (the term *"Gentile"* or *"Gentiles"* occurs some 100 times there). And so, it is not surprising that they are mentioned in the confession-chant that Paul quoted in his letter to Timothy.

WHO PREACHED TO THE "*NATIONS*"?

Who, then, preached to these "*nations*," these "Gentiles"? The past tense form of the verb "to preach," "*preached*," definitely links the preaching among the nations with the second line of the chant, which says "[God] *was manifested in the flesh*," and so it points to the preaching ministry of Christ and His apostles. If Paul wrote 1 Timothy around A.D. 65, this means that he was describing some thirty-five years of preaching to the nations, from Jesus' entrance into His public ministry up to the time Paul penned this very epistle. The New Testament tells us much about this preaching activity.

Gentiles were among the common people who heard Jesus preach, and they were in the throngs that pressed upon Him as He proclaimed all that He had come to accomplish as the Incarnate Word. "*Greeks*" (John 12:20), or Gentiles, approached Philip with the request, "*Sir, we wish to see Jesus*" (verse 21). Jesus replied that the hour had come for Him, as God manifested in the flesh, to fall into the earth and die, so that He might bring forth much fruit. (See John 12:23–24.)

There were times when Jesus appeared to share the Jewish concept that Gentiles were excluded from the covenant of promise. Did He not say that "*salvation is of the Jews*" (John 4:22 KJV, NKJV) and that He was "*sent only to the lost sheep of the house of Israel*" (Matthew 15:24)? However, the wider context of this second statement shows that there is more to the story.

Jesus said this to a woman whom Mark calls "*a Greek, a Syrophoenician by birth*" (Mark 7:26). This woman, hearing of the fame of Jesus as a preacher and healer, came to Him, brokenhearted over her demon-possessed daughter. Her request for the exorcism of the evil spirit was met with an apparently harsh refusal. Jesus said to her, "*Let the children* [the Jews] *first be fed, for it is not right to take the children's bread and throw it to the dogs* [the Gentiles]" (Mark 7:27). (The Jews regarded the Gentiles as "dogs," but their own prophets warned them that if they were spiritually complacent and unrighteous, they would become like "dogs" themselves. [See Isaiah 56:10–11.]) The woman bravely and cleverly replied, "*Yes, Lord; yet even the dogs under the table eat the children's crumbs*" (Mark 7:28). This desperate plea of the distressed Gentile woman elicited great praise from Jesus. Impressed by her reply, her persistence, and her faith, Jesus commended her as a woman of great faith and lifted the burden from her heart by assuring her that on her return, she would find her daughter whole again.

Surely, this mother will ever remain a remarkable case of faith outside Israel, and of Jesus' exceptional healing beyond the precincts of the elect nation He had deemed to be His special sphere of ministry. Other Gentiles also heard Him preach, and they were helped by His miraculous power, for had He not come, as Simeon said, to be *"a light for revelation to the Gentiles"* as well as for *"glory to thy people Israel"* (Luke 2:32)? Jesus *"went about doing good and healing all that were oppressed by the devil"* (Acts 10:38), whatever nation they came from.

Indeed, when the angel of the Lord announced the birth of Jesus, he said that His arrival as a Babe was *"good tidings of great joy, which shall be to all people"* (Luke 2:10 KJV). Then, as Jesus came to preach, He declared that *"God…loved the world,"* made up of Jews and Gentiles, and that *"whoever"* believed in Him would not perish. (See John 3:16.) At the end of Jesus' life, as He was dying by a Gentile method of death, His first convert through the sacrifice He was born to offer was the Gentile thief, doubtless a Roman dying for crimes committed against his country. (See Matthew 27:44; Luke 23:39–43.) And as Jesus was about to be received up into glory, He commissioned His disciples to go out and teach *"all nations"* (Matthew 28:19) what He had accomplished by life, lip, and libation (that is, through His incarnation, teaching, and sacrifice).

So the first answer to the question of who preached to the nations is Jesus Himself. But His disciples immediately became the next to preach. The book of Acts is filled with dramatic evidence that the apostles obeyed His Great Commission and *"preached Jesus and the resurrection"* (Acts 17:18) to Gentiles as well as to Jews, with astonishing results. While Pentecost, with its dynamic ministry of the Spirit, was confined to the apostles and to devout Jews who lived in *"every nation under heaven"* (Acts 2:5), Peter nevertheless said on that occasion that the promise of the Spirit was also *"to all that are far off, every one whom the Lord our God calls to him"* (verse 39). In his preaching, Peter stressed the incarnation of his Lord in his description of Him as *"Jesus of Nazareth, a man attested to you by God"* (Acts 2:22) who died, rose again, and was exalted on high.

Like their Master, the apostles felt the lash of the whip when they came to face the hostile Jewish rulers over their preaching in the temple of Jesus and His resurrection, resulting in about 5,000 men being converted. (See Acts 4:4.) But when Peter was arrested and interrogated, he boldly insisted, *"There is no other name under heaven given among men* [irrespective of race or religion] *by which we must be saved"* (Acts 4:12); and when he was ordered to speak no more in the name of Jesus, he replied, *"Whether it is right in the sight of God to listen to you rather than to God, you must judge; for we cannot but speak of what we have seen and heard"* (Acts 4:19–20). The opposition to the apostles' preaching continued; Stephen became the first martyr of the early church for preaching the words and works of Jesus of Nazareth. (See Acts 7.)

Paul was outstanding as an apostle who also preached the unsearchable riches of Christ to the Gentiles, but it was actually while he was on his way to capture Jews who believed in Jesus and bring them, bound, to Jerusalem—that is, to take part in this same opposition—that the Lord appeared to him and said, *"I am Jesus, whom you are persecuting"* (Acts 9:5). Jesus told Paul, through the disciple Ananias, that he was *"a chosen instrument"* to carry His name *"before the Gentiles and kings and the sons of Israel"* (Acts 9:15). As Paul, transformed by grace, commenced this commission, the Jews took counsel to kill him (see Acts 9:23)—the first of his many sufferings for the sake of Jesus' name. Like his Master, Paul found himself rejected by Jewish rulers, and thus there came about his marvelous apostleship to the Gentiles. *"Behold, we turn to the Gentiles"* (Acts 13:46), he said, and his preaching to them produced remarkable results. Peter, too, had earlier thrown off the cloak of Jewish exclusion and become a mighty preacher to the Gentiles. (See Acts 10:9–48.)

WHAT MESSAGE WAS PREACHED TO THE *"NATIONS"*?

So we have seen who the *"nations"* are, and who preached to them; let us now consider the message that was preached. Paul summed up the message of the apostles well when he wrote to the Ephesians that he had been given grace to *"preach to the Gentiles the unsearchable riches of Christ"* (Ephesians 3:8), that *"the Gentiles are fellow heirs"* with the people of Israel, *"members of the same body, and partakers of the promise in Christ Jesus through the gospel"* (verse 6). In other words, the essential message that the apostles preached to the Gentiles about Jesus was the message of *reconciliation*. Whether savage or civilized, the nations could be delivered from their sin and made part of the mystic fabric of the church of the living God. As Dummelow paraphrased the Pauline statement of Ephesians 2:11–22:

> The Gentiles were formerly cut off from Israel and from God's promises. But now Christ's death has broken down the barrier between Gentile and Jew, and reconciled both as one body to God. There are now no

strangers: all are fellow-citizens; all are part of a spiritual temple, in which God, in His Spirit dwells.[71]

As Paul made this statement, he reminded the Ephesians that in time past, as Gentiles, they were *"alienated from the commonwealth of Israel, and strangers to the covenants of promise"* (Ephesians 2:12). By so doing, he fully and fittingly described their former distinction from Jews. For countless centuries, Jews and Gentiles had been kept apart by strict religious distinctions. Jews were forbidden to eat with Gentiles. Children born of mixed marriages between Jews and Gentiles were considered to be illegitimate. Attitudes and practices like these were what caused the Jews to be so hated by Greeks and Romans, as the writings of Cicero and Seneca reveal.

However, Israel's religious distinctiveness had a wider purpose, as has been well summarized for us by Fausset:

> With all the superiority of the Gentile great world kingdoms, in military prowess, commerce, luxury, and the fine arts, Israel stood on an immense *moral* elevation above them, in the one point, *nearness to God*, and possession of His revealed will and Word....But this superiority was in order that Israel, as priests unto God, might be mediator of blessings unto all nations (Isaiah 61:6). The covenant from the first with Abraham contemplated that "in his seed all the nations of the earth should be blessed" (Genesis 22:18).[72]

In other words, Israel had been entrusted with special spiritual privileges so that it could share them with all other nations. The Gentiles may have had many advantages, as Fausset described, but their might was ultimately *carnal*, while that of Israel was *spiritual*. Gentile monarchy put its trust in princes, horses, and chariots; but Israel's trust was in the Lord. (See Psalms 20:7; 118:9.) For the Gentile, it was the arm of flesh—for Israel, the arm of the Lord. (See 2 Chronicles 32:8.) Rudyard Kipling, in his marvelous "Recessional," has these stirring stanzas:

> If, drunk with sight of power, we loose
> Wild tongues that have not Thee in awe—
> Such boastings as the Gentiles use,
> Or lesser breeds without the Law—

---

71. Dummelow, *Commentary on the Holy Bible*, 962.
72. A. R. Fausset, *Bible Cyclopaedia, Critical and Expository* (Hartford: Scranton, 1908), 250.

Lord God of Hosts, be with us yet,
Lest we forget—lest we forget!

For heathen heart that puts her trust
In reeking tube and iron shard—
All valiant dust that builds on dust,
And, guarding, calls not Thee to guard.
For frantic boast and foolish word—
Thy mercy on Thy People, Lord!

And so God, in His mercy, called one nation to receive and understand His will and Word so that they could share them with all the nations of the world.

While the Old Testament predicts salvation for all nations, the emphasis there is upon the salvation of Israel through the coming of her Messiah and of her inclusion in God's redemption scheme. Thus, even at the start of the New Testament, many, like the *"righteous and devout"* Simeon, were *"looking for the consolation of Israel"* (Luke 2:25) and, like godly Anna, were *"looking for the redemption of Jerusalem"* (verse 38). But we see God's blessings spread from the Jews to the Gentiles over the course of the New Testament.

The story of Jesus begins with the declaration that He was born to *"save his people from their sins"* (Matthew 1:21), that He was the *"horn of salvation"* raised up from the house of David for His people, whom He had come to redeem. (See Luke 1:68–71.) But although Jesus came unto His own people, the Jews, they did not receive Him as their Messiah. Jesus lamented to Jerusalem, *"How often would I have gathered your children together as a hen gathers her brood under her wings, and you would not!"* (Matthew 23:37). The Gospels are a long record of the hatred of the Jewish hierarchy toward Jesus, a hatred satisfied only when they had engineered the cruel, Gentile form of death for Him who was *"the King of the Jews"* (Matthew 27:37).

The Jews themselves, in national pride, failed to see that through them the Gentile nations were supposed to be blessed. In rejecting their Messiah, they were *"broken off"* from the olive tree, so that the Gentiles might be *"grafted in."* (See Romans 11:19–24.) Not until the times of the Gentiles are fulfilled will the times of Israel begin, with a glory eclipsing her past lost glory. *"All Israel will be saved"* (Romans 11:26), and if their rejection meant the reconciliation of the world, *"what will their acceptance mean but life from the dead?"* (verse 15). (The projected course of God's dealings with the kingdoms of this world, right up until their consummation when Christ returns as King of Kings and Lord of Lords to make all of them His own world-kingdom, is a subject of absorbing interest, but, as it is beyond the scope of the phrase we are presently considering, we must reluctantly desist from pursuing it.)

The early confession of faith we are exploring in this book was peculiarly the outcome of the Pauline churches, in which Gentiles predominated. One of the glories of the Redeemer was the way in which the preaching of His saving gospel greatly influenced those who had hitherto sat in darkness as in the shadow of death. *"Preached among the nations"* is the wonderful fulfillment of Isaiah's thrice-rejected prophecy of the Messiah's advent as a *"light to the nations"* (Isaiah 42:6; 49:6; see also Isaiah 60:3). As we consider this line from the confession-chant together with the preceding one, *"seen by angels,"* we recognize the antithesis that once existed between the angels, who were so near to the Son of God, the Lord of angels, and the Gentiles, who were so utterly *"far off"* (Ephesians 2:17) from Him. This antithesis is no more. As Ellicott summarized this widespread evangelization among those who were once aliens from the commonwealth of Israel:

> The angels now for the first time saw, and gazed on, and rejoiced in, the vision of the Godhead manifested in the glorified humanity of the Son; and what the angels gained in the beatific vision, the nations of the world obtained through the preaching of the gospel, namely, the knowledge of the endless love and the surpassing glory of Christ.[73]

It would take volumes to record the great multitudes of Gentiles who have been saved by grace since the apostolic age through the preaching of the glorious gospel of the incarnation of Christ. We can only imagine their number by comparison with the thousands of thousands and ten thousand times ten thousand of the holy angels.

And this brings us to the "preaching among the nations" in our own day. In the New Testament, the nations or Gentiles were those who were neither of Israel nor of the church, because in Christ, there is *"neither Jew nor Greek"* (Galatians 3:28). In this age of grace, the true church is composed of both Jews and Gentiles, born anew by the Holy Spirit, who are no longer known nationally but are one in Christ Jesus. God does not look down upon people and segregate them nationally. To Him, they are all alike sinners needing to be saved in the

73. Ellicott, *New Testament Commentary for Schools: St. Luke*, 226.

same way by the same Savior. *"All have sinned and fall short of the glory of God"* (Romans 3:23). Since apostolic times, a vast multitude of Gentiles no one can number has responded to the preaching of the gospel and become new creatures in Christ Jesus. Blessed be His name, I am one of them, for, as I write these lines, it is well over seventy years since I, as a lost Gentile, heard Christ preached as the One who died for my salvation, and, in an evangelistic meeting, opened the avenues of my being to Him who translated me from my darkness into His marvelous light.

It is to be questioned whether the present-day church shares the passion of the early church to preach Christ, in all His fullness, to Gentiles. In our world, millions of Gentiles (people outside the church) are waiting to hear of Him who came as the Light of the World. He is also the *light* of Israel but has been rejected as such. Before He can become her *glory* in His millennial reign, her eyes must be opened to see Him whom they pierced, and they must mourn and repent of their long, persistent rejection of Him. (See Zechariah 12:10–11.) And so, evangelistic efforts must include reaching the lost in the house of Israel; and there are a score of Jewish missions active in winning Jews for Christ. But the preponderance of Gentiles all over the earth presents a challenge the church cannot escape. She must hear the bitter cry of earth's millions: "Come and help us, for we die!" And with urgency, the church must proclaim to them, in the same words that Paul wrote to the Corinthians, *"God was in Christ, reconciling the world unto himself, not imputing their trespasses unto them; and hath committed unto us the word of reconciliation"* (2 Corinthians 5:19 kjv). Then our understanding of the *"mystery of our religion,"* summarized in Paul's confession-chant, will also rest on the Pillar of Proclamation, as it must be if it is to be built solid as the house of wisdom.

6

THE PILLAR OF BELIEF

"Believed on in the world...."
—1 Timothy 3:16

The sixth line that the apostle quoted from a hymn of faith that the church of his day chanted, *"believed on in the world,"* is not a mere repetition of the previous line, *"preached among the nations."* Rather, it shows how *believing* follows the *preaching* of the cross, which, to all who believe, becomes the power of God for salvation. (See Romans 1:16.) In his epistle to the Romans, Paul, in declaring that there is no difference between Jew or Gentile when it comes to the gospel invitation, rings the changes on *preaching* and *believing:*

> *But how are men to call upon him in whom they have not believed? And how are they to believe in him of whom they have never heard? And how are they to hear without a preacher? And how can men preach unless they are sent? As it is written, "How beautiful are the feet of those who preach good news!"...So faith comes from what is heard, and what is heard comes by the preaching of Christ.* (Romans 10:14–15, 17)

Who or what was *"believed on in the world"* up to the time Paul wrote his first epistle to Timothy? Such a question takes us back to the second line, which announces that Jesus came as God manifested in the flesh; that, as the Son of

God, He became the Son of Man for the supreme purpose of seeking and saving the lost in the world. Thus, at the heart of His incarnation was the provision of redemption for a whole world lost in the darkness of sin. From the time of Adam's transgression, the world has lain in wickedness and is more than ever buried in it: *"The whole world is in the power of the evil one"* (1 John 5:19).

It is interesting to compare what Paul said in 1 Timothy 3:16 about believing and the world with the gospel statement in John 3:16: *"God so loved the world that he gave his only Son, that whoever believes in him should not perish but have eternal life."* From the time Jesus gave the world this most wonderful summary of the good news, He has been believed on in the world by myriads who have found in Him a personal Savior from the guilt and penalty of their sin. They have proved that, in Walter Chalmers Smith's words:

> Faith alone is the master-key
> To the strait gate and narrow road;
> All others but skeleton pick-locks be.
> And you never shall pick the locks of God.[74]

While here, in the days of His flesh, Jesus predicted the magnetism of His cross when He said, *"I, when I am lifted up from the earth, will draw all men to myself"* (John 12:32). As Genevieve Irons wrote in her hymn "Drawn to the Cross":

> Drawn to the cross, which Thou hast blest,
> With healing gifts for souls distressed,
> To find in Thee my life, my rest,
> Christ Crucified, I come.

The religious leaders would not come like this to Him in order that they might have life. They found Jesus a controversial figure; they rejected His claims to deity and finally plotted His death. But, while they deliberately shut their eyes to faith, the common people heard Him gladly and believed on Him. The Pharisees themselves had to confess to one another, *"You see that you can do nothing; look, the world has gone after him"* (John 12:19). They said this because the resurrection of Lazarus from the dead had brought even Gentiles from afar to see and hear Jesus.

---

74. Walter Chalmers Smith, *Hilda Among the Broken Gods* (Glasgow: James MacLehose and Sons, 1882), 182.

When John the Baptist was put in prison, Jesus went into Galilee preaching the gospel, calling upon all and sundry to repent and believe. And before His ascension, He commissioned His disciples to go out into all the world and preach the gospel as He had to every creature—which they did, with the *"signs following"* of many people believing in the crucified, risen, and exalted Savior whom they preached. (See Mark 16:20 KJV.)

A brief word is necessary concerning two statements John made, namely, *"God so loved the world"* (John 3:16) and *"Do not love the world"* (1 John 2:15). There is, of course, no contradiction between these two phrases, for the true believer loves what God loves. When John, the Apostle of Love, told us not to love the world, he referred to *"things"* in the world, as he went on to state: *"Do not love the world or the things in the world."* The things in the world are its pleasures, pastimes, pursuits, and policies. As a sphere to live in, the world is a corrupt place; but grace can be ours to live as those who are not of this world. Those who live thus are those who *"believe"* that the Father sent His Son into the world to die for their salvation. (See John 17:14–15, 21.)

For those redeemed by the blood, the world is a shadow and the enemy's domain, seeing that the devil is the god it follows. It is the world that crucified Jesus, and it is detrimental to life and character to be too intimate with its worldly inhabitants. The world of *things* is to be treated as vapor, appearing for a little while, then vanishing away. The saint's determination should be: *"There is nothing upon earth that I desire besides thee"* (Psalm 73:25). Or, in the words of Dr. Samuel Stennett's hymn "In Vain the Giddy World Inquires":

> Lord, from this world call off my love,
> Set my affections right:
> Bid me aspire to joys above,
> And walk no more by sight.

But in the greatest text in the Bible, when John wrote of God so loving the world, it was not a world of *things* but of *persons*—a world of sinners lost and ruined by the fall; and since Christ's coming, myriads from His day down have believed in Him and found eternal life. As the result of Peter's initial preaching of Jesus of Nazareth, who was slain but whom God raised up, about 3,000 believed and were added to the church. (See Acts 2:41.) Soon after, as Peter and John proclaimed Jesus and the resurrection, the world of men was shaken, and about

5,000 of them repented of their sin, *believing* the word *preached*. (See Acts 4:4.) And so the tide of salvation flowed on and on, as Ellicott so finely put it:

> Christianity has found acceptance among widely differing nationalities. The religion of the Crucified alone among religions has a fair claim to the title of a world-religion. Its cradle was in the East, but it rapidly found a ready acceptance in the West, and in the present-day it may be said not only to exist, but to exercise a vast and ever increasing influence in all the four quarters of the globe.[75]

When Jesus was in the world, many seeing Him in human form and listening to His fearless preaching believed on Him. Seeing, they believed. But before He was received up into glory, He said to Thomas, who had insisted that seeing is believing (see John 20:25), *"Have you believed because you have seen me? Blessed are those who have not seen and yet believe"* (verse 29). In other words, *believing is seeing*. *"Without having seen him you love him; though you do not now see him you believe in him and rejoice with unutterable and exalted joy"* (1 Peter 1:8). Since Jesus' ascension, countless myriads, whose eyes never gazed upon that radiant form of His, have been saved by faith and *"endured as seeing Him who is invisible"* (Hebrews 11:27). Under grace, repentant hearts are saved by faith, which is *"the assurance of things hoped for, the conviction of things not seen"* (Hebrews 11:1). As Hartley Coleridge bid us to remember in his poem "The Just Shall Live by Faith":

> Think not the faith by which the just shall live
> Is a dead creed, a map correct of heaven,
> Far less a feeling fond and fugitive,
> A thoughtless gift, withdrawn as soon as given.
> It is an affirmation and an act
> That bids eternal truth be present fact.

It would seem as if the church has forgotten her marching orders to go out into an unbelieving world, preaching the gospel of God loving the world, of Jesus dying for the sins of the world, and of the Holy Spirit being ever present in the world, convincing it of its sin. Is not the evangelistic spirit the emanation of the whole Godhead? The Christian church is essentially a missionary institution, with the obligation of calling upon people everywhere in the world to repent and turn to the Savior. All within her fold—those who have *"believed on"* Jesus

---

75. Ellicott, *New Testament Commentary for Schools: St. Luke*, 226.

while *"in the world"*—should never rest until they hear other smitten souls cry, *"I believe; help my unbelief!"* (Mark 9:24). How apt are the lines of Faber in the hymn "O Gift of Gifts!":

> How can they live, how will they die,
> How bear the cross of grief,
> Who have not yet the light of faith,
> The courage of belief?

Never cease to praise God if you are among the number in this world, and the world beyond, who rest upon the Pillar of Belief, who have *believed* in Him who became flesh and died for your redemption.

7

THE PILLAR OF GLORIFICATION

"Taken up in glory."
—1 Timothy 3:16

With this final pillar, the foundation becomes complete. As commentators have observed, when viewed in its entirety, our confession-chant arches from Bethlehem (*"manifested in the flesh"*) to the heights of heavenly majesty: *"Taken up in glory"*! In between, the Savior is seen as the object of angelic contemplation and the subject of apostolic preaching, and He is acclaimed as the One vindicated not only in His spirit but also in the hearts of all who believe in Him. But the first and last pillars of divine wisdom supporting the temple of our Christian faith are those of the incarnation and the ascension/glorification of our Lord—His descent from heaven to earth to finish the work of redemption, and then His ascent to heaven from earth as the glorious Victor, carrying with Him the triumphs of His conquest over the devil, sin, and death. One translation of this last line of the hymn of the early church is thus: "Who, at the end of His ministry, was taken up into glory."

We read in the book of Judges that the house of Dagon, god of the Philistines, was held up by two great pillars. When poor, blind Samson was brought in from prison so his captors could make sport of him, he was placed between these pillars. Taking hold of one pillar with his right hand and the other with his left,

131

with God-restored muscular power, he *"bowed with all his might"* and crumbled those pillars into pieces as small as matchwood. The house quickly fell, killing over 3,000 idolaters, with Samson himself perishing with his enemies. (See Judges 16:25–30.)

But no Samson, religious or otherwise, can destroy the temple of truth. The two massive pillars of Incarnation and Glorification upon which the spiritual house is built are eternally secure. That Jesus came from above, and that He returned to His original abode, are twin facts that remain intact, despite the apostasy of our age. The glorification of Jesus as He ascended on high was the seal of heaven. It showed that the mission He came to accomplish as He took upon Himself the likeness of our flesh was perfectly realized.

A HEAVENLY RECEPTION FOR THE MIGHTY VICTOR!

What a blessed conclusion this is of the ancient triumph song! After thirty-three years in the far-off country of this earth of ours, in which Jesus lived a sinless life and ultimately died for a prodigal world, He returned to His Father's house, in which there was no elder brother to vent his jealousy over the loving and lavish reception accorded God's beloved Son. (See Luke 15:28–30.) It was right that all heaven should make merry; for, after being dead, He was now alive forevermore and was coming home a mighty Victor o'er His foes with the keys of death and hell dangling at His waist—trophies of His redemptive task perfectly accomplished.

What a court reception that must have been! Who was at the gate of heaven as Jesus entered? Certainly, His Father was there to welcome Him, speaking the treasured phrase with added meaning: "You are My beloved Son, with whom I am well pleased." It was Jesus' express desire to return to the Father and to behold the glory given to Him by the Father before the world began. This is also His personal glory that the saints are to behold. (See John 17:5, 24.) So, all the saints of past ages, who looked for the redemption of Israel before His birth, must have been raptured as they saw Jesus and entered heaven with Him as the Redeemer efficacious to emancipate from the tyranny of their sin all who believe.

But there were others at His reception, as well. The statement that Jesus was *"taken up to glory"* raises the question, "Who took Him up?" The spiritual "Swing Low, Sweet Chariot" may give us the answer in the stanza that says:

I looked over Jordan, and what did I see,
Coming for to carry me home?
A band of angels coming after me,
Coming for to carry me home.

Whatever share the angels may have in our own translation to heaven, it is evident they were associated with Jesus in His ascension, and that the vast celestial host surrounding the throne of God must have joined in the welcome their Creator received on His triumphal entry into heaven. If the angels sang a song of such timeless beauty at the incarnation of Jesus, who can imagine what they must have sung upon His ascension! Perhaps the hymnist Cousin has captured something of the spirit of this angelic adoration:

To Thee and to Thy Christ, O God,
We sing, we ever sing;
For He hath crushed beneath His rod
The world's proud rebel king.
He plunged in His imperial strength
To gulfs of darkness down;
He brought His trophy up at length,
The foiled usurper's crown.

JESUS WAS HONORED WITH MANY TITLES

But Jesus did not receive just praise and adoration from His Father, the redeemed saints, and the holy angels. He was honored upon His ascension with many titles that make up the *"name which is above every name"* (Philippians 2:9) that He received after He humbled Himself and God highly exalted Him. The inspired writers of Scripture have recorded these titles for us in various places and so have given us a glimpse into the heavenly honors and offices that our ascended Lord enjoys.

We noted in chapter 5 that Stephen was the first Christian martyr. Luke tells us that as Stephen was being stoned to death, he cried out, *"I see the heavens opened, and the Son of Man standing at the right hand of God"* (Acts 7:56). Stephen is the only person in the New Testament to utter this title apart from Jesus Himself, who used it some forty times. As Stephen looked into heaven, he saw Jesus in His human form—God manifested in glorified flesh—and in this form

Jesus will ever remain the perfect representative Man. Dummelow's *Commentary* says that the title *Son of Man*

> probably designates our Lord as the ideal or representative man, "the man in whom human nature was most fully and deeply realized, and who was the most complete exponent of its capacities, warm and broad in His sympathies, ready to minister and suffer for others, sharing to the full the needs and deprivations which are the common lot of humanity, but conscious at the same time of the dignity and greatness of human nature, and destined ultimately to exalt it to unexampled majesty and glory."[76]

The prophet Ezekiel, captive by the river Chebar, had visions of God as the heavens opened. His captivity did not prevent him from receiving a captivating revelation of the glory of God! Among the visions granted the imprisoned prophet was one in which there was *"the likeness of a throne,…and seated above the likeness of a throne was a likeness as it were of a human form"* (Ezekiel 1:26). How prophetic this vision was of the glorified humanity of the Man Christ Jesus after His return to heaven to assume dominion of all things!

Seeing Jesus received into heaven as the Son of Man was an utterly new experience for the angels. They had already watched saints enter heaven with the human bodies in which they had lived, bodies transformed in their ascent to the abode of God and the angels. Both Enoch and Elijah were translated directly, without tasting death. Both Moses and Elijah came to the Mount of Transfiguration in their glorified but recognizable bodies. But the Babe born at Bethlehem, who became the Man crucified at Calvary, was God manifested in the flesh; and now the wonder among the angels, who before had never looked on God, was to see God the Son for the first time, and that with a human face.

To the celestial host, it was the marvel of marvels to see those hands, once pierced with nails, now holding the scepter of authority, ruling over all, and having all events under His control. They also saw those human feet, once nailed to a bloody cross, representing the purchase price of His saving grace, and thus tuned their harps to praise Him. Through all eternity, the object of universal worship and adoration in heaven will be that of the wonderful sight of humanity's dust glorified and seated on a throne as the Son of Man.

---

76. Dummelow, *A Commentary on the Holy Bible*, 654.

It is not generally understood that the return to glory of Jesus, as the Man of Sorrows acquainted with human grief (see Isaiah 53:3), whom angels acclaimed at His ascension, brought about a change in the composition of the Trinity, which, before the incarnation, was made up of God who is Spirit, the Holy Spirit, and God the Son. All three had the same essence, the same elements of personality, but were devoid of a person, or body, such as God the Son assumed when He left heaven and became the Son of Man. What form Their eternal essence was clothed with we are not told!

But this we do know—with Christ's ascension and return to the Holy Cabinet, there is a member of it who, although He became God manifested in the flesh and the One who was touched with the feeling of human infirmities, went back to heaven as the One well-qualified to assume the office of the Great High Priest in order to make intercession for those humans on earth with whom He was closely identified. No wonder the angelic host, and likewise the redeemed host in glory, exclaim, *"Worthy is the lamb who was slain"* (Revelation 5:12). The Trinity now has a member who is God in glorified human form; and thus, it is encouraging to our faith, as we linger amid the shadows, to know that we have an Advocate at the right hand of God who was tempted in all points as we are, but who was victorious and who is ever ready to make us the recipients of His victory.

In speaking of Jesus as our *Priest* and *Advocate*, we have already begun to mention some of the many other titles the biblical writers gave to the ascended Jesus. *Priest* is one of the most meaningful and comforting of these. When He was received up into glory, our Savior entered into His priestly ministry, which has continued for almost two millennia and will not cease until all His saints are gathered to Him. He is now our Great High Priest, who passed into the heavens. (See Hebrews 4:14.) There He pleads His sacrificial death on our behalf, makes intercession for us, and sympathizes, succors, and sanctifies His redeemed ones. Because of His willingness to become manifested in flesh, and to remain in the flesh even in heaven as the Son of Man, He became vitally associated with many human infirmities and is thus able to present our cause. (See Hebrews 4:15.) As our priestly Intercessor, Jesus is ever willing to make requests of the Father on our behalf, on the basis of His perfect sacrifice for our salvation. (See Hebrews 7:21–25; 9:26.)

Because He is alive forevermore, His people share His risen life; and in glory, He sees *"the fruit of the travail of his soul"* (Isaiah 53:11) while on earth in the regeneration, sanctification, perseverance, and glorification of all those in His beloved family. As their Priest, He lives to pray for them, console them, and watch over them, and to execute all the purposes of the Father concerning the church He purchased with His blood to be representatives of His holiness.

Further, when Jesus entered into His priestly ministry, it was not to create a priesthood within His church or to have its individual pastors and ministers serve as priests. Rather, it was that all true believers should become *"kings and priests unto God"* (Revelation 1:6 KJV), or *"a kingdom and priests to our God"* (Revelation 5:10); *"a royal priesthood"* (1 Peter 2:9); *"priests of God and of Christ"* (Revelation 20:6). Thus, the Old Testament revelation that Israel was *"a kingdom of priests"* (Exodus 19:6) was transferred to the spiritual Israel, the church.

Since the glorified Christ is princely as well as priestly, all of His own are to share in His dominion over the earth. It is to be questioned, however, whether all the children of God on this side of heaven realize their priceless position and privileges as a company of worshipping priests, namely, that they can have boldness to enter the Holiest of All by a new and living way through the veil (see Hebrews 10:19–22); that they have direct access to the Father by the Spirit (see Ephesians 2:18); and that theirs is the responsibility of offering up both *spiritual* and *living* sacrifices (see 1 Peter 2:5; Romans 12:1), and also of offering up prayers and praises (see Hebrews 13;15; Revelation 8:3). Would that more believers in the church today would realize how they share in the ministry of Jesus, their ascended Priest!

In connection with the priesthood of Jesus, the writer to the Hebrews said, *"He had to be made like his brethren in every respect, so that he might become a merciful and faithful high priest"* (Hebrews 2:17). This verse reveals another title of the ascended Jesus, and it is again a most comforting one: *Brother*. Born into a typical, godly Jewish home, Jesus came to know all about human relationships, seeing He was brought up with brothers and sisters born to Joseph and Mary after His own wondrous birth. Thus, when He entered His public ministry at about thirty years of age and gathered disciples around Himself, He said that all who obeyed the will of His Father were His brothers and sisters. (See Mark 3:35.) Thus, in a most effective way, He spiritualized these close associations of family life with which He had had intimate experience.

Now that Jesus Himself is in heaven, He does not receive us as His common subjects but as His brothers and sisters who have a blood relationship with Him brought about through His sacrifice on our behalf. Has the reality of this privileged association gripped your heart? Jesus calls Himself your *Brother*! Why should we charge our hearts with unnecessary care and concern when we have in Jesus One who wears our nature, whose heart beats in union with ours, and whose brotherly love toward us never fails? During the widespread famine in Egypt, Joseph supplied his brothers with all they needed; and our heavenly Joseph's fraternal kindness ever corresponds to our need. As we approach the throne of grace, then, let us remember that our Brother occupies it and that He will withhold no good thing from us. In the words of the hymn "Jesus, Who Passed the Angels By":

> Our nearest Friend, our Brother now,
> Is He to whom the angels bow;
> They join with us to praise His name,
> But we the nearest interest claim.

He is, indeed, our nearest *Friend*, in addition to being our Brother. While on earth, He said that all who followed His commands were His friends. (See John 15:14–15.) He is the Friend who loves at all times and who sticks closer than a brother (see Proverbs 17:17; 18:24), the One who bears our sins and griefs and to whom we can take everything in prayer—what a Friend we have in Jesus! And His friendly ability to help us is one of the joys that was set before Him when He endured the cross and despised its shame. (See Hebrews 12:2.)

In addition to these titles, which express the consoling personal associations of Jesus with those who are His as members of His body, there are others of a more official character that the New Testament also takes cognizance of in relation to His being received up into glory. One of these is *Forerunner*, which is found only in Hebrews 6:20. In classical usage, "forerunner" implies one who goes before, as a scout to reconnoiter, or as a herald to announce the coming of a king or to make ready the way for a royal journey. Commenting on this title of Jesus, Professor A. B. Bruce said that the Greek word from which "*forerunner*" is translated, *prodromos*, "expresses the whole essential difference between the Christian and Levitical religions—between the religion that brings men nigh to God, and the religion that kept or left men standing at a distance."[77] The Jewish high priest entered the Holy of Holies in the temple by himself one day in the year, but only as the people's representative, not as a forerunner for any who might dare to follow him. But when Jesus entered the heavenly Holy of Holies by

---

77. Alexander Balmain Bruce, *The Epistle to the Hebrews* (Edinburgh: T. & T. Clark, 1899), 11.

His own blood at His ascension, He went beyond the veil as our Forerunner and likewise as our Leader, taking us there with Him. (See Hebrews 9:24; 10:19–22.) Before He left His own, He assured them that He was going to prepare a place for them. (See John 14:2–3.)

While we use the term *forerunner* also of John the Baptist, the Gospels do not describe him as such, but rather as the messenger sent before the face of the Lord to "prepare His way" (see Malachi 3:1; Luke 3:4) and to exhort the people to "*make his paths straight*" (Luke 3:4). Thus, in a true sense, John was his Lord's forerunner, just as Jesus was his forerunner (and ours) into the heavenly Holy of Holies. Going before His own into the heavenly abode, Jesus had no need to reconnoiter it as a scout, seeing that He had lived there through the past eternity, before His incarnation. He was the One who went before to announce His great victory, to open the way for the blood-washed to enter the Holy of Holies, and to act as their Representative.

The New Testament also describes the ascended Jesus as our *Mediator*. The term *mediator* is from a root meaning "middle." Such a person in certain human relationships is the middleman, the go-between, who intervenes between two parties for peace and unites parties at variance. This further expressive metaphor, applied to the exalted Savior in the New Testament, occurs in relation to Jesus as the "*one mediator between God and men*" (1 Timothy 2:5) and as the Mediator of a "*new*" or "*better*" covenant. (See Hebrews 8:6; 9:15; 12:24.) Throughout Scripture, mediation, in which God deals with man not directly but through the interposition of another, is fairly common. Paul described Moses as the mediator of the law. (See Galatians 3:19–20 KJV, NKJV.) In intercessory prayer, such mediation is the privilege of all the saints. (See, for example, James 5:16.) But Jesus is our heavenly Middleman who presents our prayers, our praises, and our persons to God through Himself.

In the use of the term as applied to Jesus, there was never, and can never be, any disagreement on God's side to appease and make amendable to man. Variances to deal with are all on the human side. As the embodiment of God's interposing oath (see Hebrews 6:17), Jesus interposed Himself as Mediator between God and us. Is this not our plea at the throne of grace, our song in the house of our pilgrimage, and our confidence in the prospect of death, that Jesus is our Mediator?

Because of His holiness and righteousness, God must ever be the eternal enemy of sin. It is the abominable thing He hates, and He can never be reconciled to it but must look upon it with abhorrence. How, then, can He receive, bless, and commune with sinners like ourselves? Only through a Mediator. Jesus, as the Son of God, knows all about the divine side and ever honors all the Father's perfections. But, as the One who became the Son of Man, He also knows all that there is to know from the human side, and He makes man acceptable to God through His own glorious righteousness and finished work of redemption.

In this way, as Fausset noted in his *Bible Dictionary* under the term "mediator," Jesus functions like the *"umpire"* Job wished for in his dealings with God, *"who might lay his hand upon us both"* (Job 9:33), "in token of his power to adjudicate." The only Umpire to whose authoritative decision both God and ourselves are equally amendable is the God-Man, who is on a level with both God and man. He never fails to reconcile the repentant, believing sinner to God. Again, on God's part, He has no need of reconciliation to man. And sinners can be reconciled to Him only through the death of His Son.

A further office of our ascended Lord in heaven, already noted above in our discussion of the changed composition of the Trinity, is that of *Advocate*—"We have an advocate with the Father" (1 John 2:1). The simple, original meaning of "advocate" is that of one called to help, or one who pleads in favor of, and is the representative of, another. As far back as the book of Job was written, in which the friends were criticized for their failures as *"miserable comforters"* (Job 16:2), *advocate* already carried the twofold meaning of one who comforts or exhorts and one who is appealed to as a proxy or as an attorney called to our aid.

During His earthly ministry, Jesus was God's Advocate with men, pleading God's cause with them and seeking to win them for Him. Now He is our Advocate in heaven; for by His sacrifice, He returned to heaven, there to appear in the presence of God for us, pleading for us against every argument of Satan. *"He always lives to make intercession for* [us]" (Hebrews 7:25). Ellicott's comment on 1 John 2:1, *"We have an advocate with the Father,"* is enlightening:

> The Redeemer, the Word made flesh, and reascended with His human nature, is that part of the Deity which assures us of the ever-active vitality of divine love. If the justice of God is connected most with the Father, the mercy is pledged by the Son. He has exalted our nature, undertaken our interests, presents our prayers, and will one day be surrounded by the countless millions of His human brothers whom He has rescued, wearing the same nature as Himself. He is represented as continuing

our Advocate, because otherwise His work might appear a mere separate earthly manifestation; "righteous" because Christ, the only blameless example of human nature, can alone intercede for it with God.[78]

It is thus we can sing with loving, grateful hearts, in the words of the old hymn by Anne Steele:

> Look up, my soul, with cheerful eye,
> See where the great Redeemer stands;
> The glorious Advocate on high,
> With precious incense in His hands.

Not only did John say in his first epistle that in Jesus *"we have an advocate with the Father,"* but in his gospel he applied the same term (sometimes translated as *"Comforter"* or *"Counselor"* in English Bibles) to the Holy Spirit. As Jesus was about to leave His disciples and ultimately return to heaven, He said He did not want to leave them *"desolate"* or *"comfortless"* (KJV) or *"orphans"* (NKJV), so He promised, *"I will pray the Father, and he will give you another Counselor [Advocate],...even the Spirit of truth"* (John 14:16–17). It is interesting to observe that the simple word *"another"* has two possible meanings in the original, namely, "one of the same kind" or "another of a different kind." Needless to say, Jesus used the word in the first sense when He said that He would send "another" Advocate like Himself, who would not be recognized by an unspiritual world but who would be lovingly received by believers. (See John 14:17.) The Holy Spirit would constantly testify to them of their unseen Lord, who, although absent in body, would still be present with them by His Spirit.

The ideas embodied in the role of advocate apply, then, both to the Spirit and to the Savior, as the latter intercedes with God for us above (see Hebrews 7:25), while the Spirit intercedes in us below (see Romans 8:26–27). Thus, although Jesus is no longer on earth, since the Holy Spirit is His Spirit, He is still with us while absent in body. We have the Advocate within to convict us when we commit sin, and another Advocate in heaven to plead His efficacious blood on our behalf. As Alfred H. Vine wrote in his hymn to the Holy Spirit "O Breath of God, Breathe on Us Now":

> Christ is our Advocate on high;
> Thou art our Advocate within.

---

78. Ellicott, *New Testament Commentary for Schools: St. Luke*, 202.

O plead the truth, and make reply
To every argument of sin.

Thomas Binney wrote in a similar vein in his awe-inspiring hymn "Eternal Light!":

There is a way for man to rise
To that sublime abode:
An offering and a sacrifice,
A Holy Spirit's energies,
An Advocate with God.

And so all the ideas included in this office of Advocate apply both to the Holy Spirit and to Jesus. Since an advocate is one who pleads in favor of another as his representative, we are doubly blessed in our twin divine Advocates. Yes, in the goodness of God, we have these two wonderful Advocates.

A final title of the ascended Jesus is *King*. Not only is Jesus in glory *"the head over all things for the church"* (Ephesians 1:22), but those hands of His, once pierced by nails, now hold the scepter of universal empire. All power in heaven and on earth is His. (See Matthew 28:18.) *"The government"* is *"upon his shoulder"* (Isaiah 9:6). He has *"the keys of Death and Hades"* (Revelation 1:18), and so *"[He] opens and no one shall shut"* and *"shuts and no one opens"* (Revelation 3:7). By Him, the crucified King, *"kings reign, and rulers decree what is just"* (Proverbs 8:15); and *"he does according to his will in the host of heaven and among the inhabitants of the earth"* (Daniel 4:35).

When He returns to earth, it will be the seat of His kingdom in its length and breadth as He fashions the kingdoms of this world into the kingdom of His own and of His Father. (See Revelation 11:15.) What a blissful era that will be when every enemy shall be put under His feet. (See 1 Corinthians 15:25.) The loving hand of Jesus, raised in blessing over the heads of His children, now controls every event. This is man's day, and the world appears to be generally Christless, yet He rules over it by His power; He rules in the church by His Word; and He rules in the heart of the believer by His Spirit. Amid all that oppresses and depresses, the triumph of faith is this: "He reigns." In the words of Charles Wesley's hymn "Rejoice, the Lord Is King":

His kingdom cannot fail,
He rules o'er earth and heav'n;

> The keys of death and hell
> Are to our Jesus giv'n:
> Lift up your heart, lift up your voice!
> Rejoice, again I say, rejoice!

There are those who assert that nowhere in Scripture is Jesus called the King of His followers. But Pilate asked Jesus, "*So you are a king?*" and He answered, "*For this I was born*" (John 18:37). There is also the interesting phrase in Revelation 15:3 (KJV), "*King of saints.*" While more recent translations adopt the reading "*King of the ages*" or "*King of the nations,*" yet somehow one loves the phrase as given in the King James Version, and to sing: "The King of Love My Shepherd Is."

All believers who are born anew by the Holy Spirit are saints, but some are more saintly than others. The difference in the degree of practical sanctification depends on the kingship or lordship of Jesus in the heart and life. When He is given the throne of a life, of the increase of His rule in such a life there is no end (see Isaiah 9:7), for the path of such a saint shines "*brighter and brighter until full day*" (Proverbs 4:18). The personal question is: If you claim to be a Christian, have you given your Savior His coronation as King over all that you are and have? Remember, He was born not only as Savior but also as Christ the Lord!

Our reflection on the titles and offices of Jesus in heaven has shown us His intimate identification with our humanity and with human relationships. He came to earth as our Immanuel—God *with* us—and now in heaven He is God *for* us, exercising His character as Son of Man, Brother, Friend, and Forerunner, and fulfilling His offices of Mediator, Advocate, High Priest, and King for the welfare of His church and the world. Isaac Watts wrote fittingly in "Dearest of All the Names Above":

> Till God in human flesh I see,
> My thoughts no comfort find;
> The holy, just, and sacred Three
> Are terrors to my mind.

> But if Immanuel's face appear,
> My hope, my joy begins;
> His name forbids my slavish fear,
> His grace removes my sins.

THE MINISTRY OF THE ASCENDED JESUS TO ESTABLISH AND BUILD HIS CHURCH

Our reflections on the climactic phrase of the confession-chant about "[God] *manifested in the flesh*," namely, that Jesus was *"taken up in glory,"* will not be complete until we have considered what Jesus did from His heavenly position of authority to establish and build up His body, the church. Paul quoted from Psalm 68:18 when he came to emphasize the ministry gifts of the now exalted Savior: *"When he ascended on high he led a host of captives, and he gave gifts to men"* (Ephesians 4:8). Bishop Horne's commentary on the Psalms, written well over a century ago, has this paragraph on the prophetic significance of the verse that Paul quoted:

> The psalmist, in the preceding verse, had declared Sion to be the habitation of Jehovah. In this verse is described the majesty and magnificence of his appearance there, as a mighty conqueror of the enemies of his people, riding upon the cherubim, as in a triumphal chariot, with all the hosts of heaven, as it were, in his retinue. Thus God descended on Sinai with the fire, the cloud, and the glory; thus he manifested himself, when taking possession of "the holy place" prepared for him in Sion...and in some such manner we may suppose king Messiah to have entered heaven at his ascension, when he went up in the clouds, with power and great glory, and all the attendant spirits joined his train, rejoicing to minister to their Lord, and increase the pomp and splendor of that glorious day.[79]

And so we can see why Paul would appeal to this Scripture to describe the ministry of the ascended Jesus. Let us consider in more detail how our exalted Lord *"led a host of captives"* and *"gave gifts to men."*

First, what exactly are we to understand by the action of the Conqueror in leading a host of captives? That it was an action definitely related to the ascension is evident from the way it is connected with it: *"When he ascended...he led."* Arthur Way's translation of the Pauline passage reads: "He went up to heaven's height; He led captive a train of vanquished foes." The usual explanation of this phrase is that the vanquished foes of Jesus were the devil, sin, death, and the curse, which He led, as it were, in a victorious procession as sign of His destruction of such enemies—that these were the evil principalities and powers that He completely stripped of authority by His death and resurrection, and He now

---

79. George Horne, *A Commentary on the Book of Psalms* (New York: Griffin and Rudd, 1813), 270.

made a public example of them. (See Colossians 2:15.) These powers of darkness had held Him up to contempt (see Hebrews 6:6), but now, as Ellicott described it:

> Taking…his metaphor from a Roman triumph, St. Paul represents Him as passing in triumphal majesty up the sacred way to the eternal gates, with the powers of evil bound as captives behind His chariot before the eyes of men and angels.[80]

We feel, however, that there is a further aspect to the work of this mighty Conqueror in leading a band of captives that have been vanquished by His power. When He ascended on high, as the conqueror of death He marshaled all the saints in paradise together and led them to heaven, their eternal abode in God's immediate presence. These were *"prisoners of hope"* (Zechariah 9:12), the saints of past ages who lived and died on earth up to the time of Jesus' resurrection and ascension, who had been in a heavenly state of captivity in paradise. As the terms *heaven* and *paradise* are often confused, a further explanation is in order.

Modern theology may maintain a seeming attitude of reverent agnosticism regarding the state of the departed, but we believe the Bible grants us sufficient light on their eternal abode and bliss. Our prayerful and careful study of Scripture prompts us to affirm that *Sheol*, or its corresponding term, *Hades*, represented the sphere of the dead in general, and that up to the time of our Lord's ascension, this abode had its two divisions—*paradise* for the righteous, and *hell* for all who had died without God and without hope. (See Ephesians 2:12.) All in this unseen world were alive and conscious, with the full exercise of their faculties, such as memory.

Poets have loved to employ their art in describing the bliss of the onetime paradise as if it were the promised heaven for the children of God. For instance, we have John Milton's magnificent epic *Paradise Lost*. There are also Faber's verses: "O Paradise! O Paradise! Who doth not crave for rest?" But the truth is that the paradise of the New Testament was never lost and was not the sphere of eternal rest. It was not identical with heaven. Nor was it a temporal abode of the saints, a kind of intermediate state where they lived between their death and the coming again of Jesus to earth. Nor was it a purgatory, in which the departed were purified in order to make them fit for heaven. Rather, as John Wesley declared in one

---

80. Charles Ellicott, *The New Testament Commentary for Schools: Colossians, Thessalonians, and Timothy* (London: Cassell, Petter, Galpin & Co., 1879), 40.

of his sermons, "Paradise is not heaven. It is, indeed, if we may be allowed the expression, the antechamber of heaven."

The dying thief, believing the dying Savior to be a King, prayed that He would remember him when He came into His kingdom. What answer did Jesus give the repentant thief? He did not say, "Truly, I say to you, today you will be with Me in heaven," but *"Truly, I say to you, today you will be with me in Paradise"* (Luke 23:43). A synonym of paradise is *"Abraham's bosom."* Our Lord referred to that place as the happy sphere where Lazarus the beggar found himself after his death. (See Luke 16:22.) It was quite natural for Jews to represent Abraham as welcoming his righteous descendants to the joys of paradise. The figure of *"bosom"* implies reclining next to him. The rich man who went to hell instead called on Abraham for mercy and help, but not on God, to whom he could not cry.

After His own death, Jesus went to paradise. During the three days our Lord's body was in the grave, He Himself was in paradise—and what a welcome He must have had! Could this have been the period when He *"went and preached to the spirits in prison"* (1 Peter 3:19), assuring those in paradise of their impending release at His ascension and, at the same time, conveying a solemn message to the doomed in hell, the other division of Sheol, regarding their ultimate abode—the lake of fire? (See Revelation 20:15.) And so when Jesus *"led a host of captives"* on high at His ascension, He was gathering the saints of past ages together and bringing them to where they could become part of the church triumphant in heaven, together with all those who would believe in Him after His resurrection and ascension.

It is significant that in His message of comfort at the Last Supper to His disciples, who were downcast because He was talking about His death, Jesus cheered their troubled hearts, assuring them that He was going to prepare a place for them, not in paradise but in the Father's spacious home—the heaven He left for earth at His incarnation. Our ultimate destination is then eternally settled—*"that where I am you may be also"* (John 14:3)—and Jesus' ascension is the seal of such a hope. Our blessed assurance is that when we come to cross the swelling tide, we are to be received by Jesus Himself, as His children, as He ushers us into His glory. Did He not promise, *"I will come again and will take you to myself"* (John 14:3)? If it is a great honor to be received at the court of an earthly potentate or king, what an inestimable privilege it will be to be received by the King of Kings!

When Stephen was dying a terrible death by stoning, he turned his blood-stained, angel-like face to heaven and prayed, *"Lord Jesus, receive my spirit"* (Acts 7:59); and after praying for those who had murdered him, he fell asleep. A remarkable feature of Stephen's last moments, as he looked up steadfastly into heaven and saw the glory of God, was the posture of his Lord, for whom he was being martyred. This most faithful witness beheld Jesus through the opened heavens *"standing at the right hand of God"* (Acts 7:56), not *seated* at the right hand of the Father, where the Gospels tell us He was enthroned after He was *"taken up into heaven"* (Mark 16:19; see also, for example, Matthew 26:64). The newly ascended Lord rose from His throne and was standing, ready with His outstretched, nail-pierced hand, to welcome into eternal bliss the first martyr in the church He had founded. (See Acts 7:54–60.)

In this age of grace, then, when a child of God dies, he does not go to paradise, or Abraham's bosom, but to be with Christ, which is far better. *"Away from the body and at home with the Lord"* (2 Corinthians 5:8). When Jesus entered heaven at His ascension, He resumed His original eternal position at the right hand of the Father, the *"Majesty on high"* (Hebrews 1:3). When Jesus returns, as He said He would, He will bring all His saints presently with Him to accompany Him—*"through Jesus, God will bring with him those who have fallen asleep"* (1 Thessalonians 4:14). Positionally, we are already seated *"in the heavenly places in Christ Jesus"* (Ephesians 2:6). And so our prayer should be the one in the hymn "Lord Jesus, Are We One with Thee?":

> O teach us, Lord, to know and own
> This wondrous mystery,
> That Thou with us art truly one,
> And we are one with Thee.

The practical application of the foregoing is not hard to recognize. If we profess to be in Christ Jesus and already seated with Him in the heavenly places, it is incumbent upon us to *"seek the things that are above"* (Colossians 3:1). Our present attitude should be that of habitually looking at the Lord Jesus—what He was in His ancient glory, what He became for us as the result of His incarnation, and what He now is—as well as what we will soon be with Him. In the words of Robert Seagrave's hymn:

> Rise, my soul, and stretch thy wings,
> Thy better portion trace;

Rise from transitory things,
Toward Heaven, thy native place.

But, in His ascension, Jesus did not just establish the church triumphant by gathering the saints of past ages together to enjoy eternal fellowship with the saints of this age in heaven. He also established the church militant on earth by providing what was needed to build it. He not only *"led a host of captives"* but also *"gave gifts to men."* And His gifts to men were men-as-gifts: apostles, prophets, evangelists, pastors, and teachers, whose gifts were for use in the expansion of His church. (See Ephesians 4:11–12.) Those who are ministers of His gifts are themselves gifts from Jesus to His church.

While He was among His disciples, Jesus revealed His wonderful design to build His church—*"I will build my church"* (Matthew 16:18). This magnificent expression regarding Himself occurs nowhere else in the Gospels. He called His church *His own*, His own glorious body! He became flesh and died so that He might bring such a church into being. It is important to notice that when Jesus revealed His purpose, He did not say that He would build His church on Peter but rather upon what Peter had just confessed. The Master asked His disciple what he thought of His life and claims; and, inspired by the Holy Spirit, Peter replied, in effect, "You are the Messiah, the Son of God." (See Matthew 16:16.) It is on this rock that Jesus, as God manifested in the flesh, built His church. Similarly, in Paul's message to the Ephesian elders, he urged them to *"care for the church of God which he obtained with the blood of his own Son"* (Acts 20:28). When the building is ultimately completed, Jesus will present it to Himself as "His glorious Bride, having no stain nor wrinkle, nor any such thing, that she might be holy and flawless" (Ephesians 5:17, Arthur Way's translation). The incarnation, then, and all that was accomplished by it, became the foundation of the church that Jesus said He would build—and build in such a way that the gates of hell, or the powers of darkness, would never be able to prevail against it. (See Matthew 16:18 kjv.) When Jesus ascended, He sent the ministry gifts needed to build the church on this foundation.

We distinguish between the visible organization and the invisible organism of the church. One can be a member of a church—an organization known as such—yet not be a member of the unseen church, which is His body. The gates of hell have certainly prevailed against the church as a visible and, in many cases, a human-developed organization. That is why there are so many branches of the church that are contrary in belief and practice. Even today, the organizational church is "by schisms rent asunder, by heresies distressed." But against the true, unseen church that Jesus would build, no subtle, satanic force can prevail. Between His resurrection and ascension, Jesus spent forty days with His chosen disciples, during which period He fully instructed them as to their share in assisting Him in the building of His church, their witness in the world, and the message they should unashamedly proclaim by the power of the Spirit. (See Acts 1:3.)

When the promise of the Father regarding the Holy Spirit coming upon the church waiting in Jerusalem was fulfilled, on the historic day of Pentecost, the apostles were greatly used in the immediate enlargement of the church, as about 3,000 souls were added—not to a visible structure but to the invisible temple, which is His body. What were the necessary qualifications for inclusion in His church? There had to be the glad and willing acceptance of the message Peter preached concerning Jesus as the prophesied, miracle-working, crucified, risen, and glorified Savior. There had to be a genuine and deep repentance of sin and then submission to baptism, which represented identification with Jesus in His death, burial, and resurrection. By these personal acts, men and women were added to His church, or joined to the Lord by the regeneration of the Spirit.

The ascension gifts of Jesus for the building up of His body reveal the bounty of heaven for His church on earth. All such bestowal of these different gifts was, and is, an act of grace. *"He gave"* (Ephesians 4:8): the original pronoun *He* is emphatic, implying that He, and He alone, is the ascended Head and Representative of humanity. He gave apostles, prophets, evangelists, pastors, and teachers. In all Paul's references to the gifts of the Spirit, there is the same general idea: first of one body, and then of the one Spirit, guiding and animating it through various ministries. Again, all who are appointed to these ministries are thus gifts of the Holy Spirit.

When Jesus *"ascended on high,"* He *"gave gifts to men"* (Ephesians 4:8). Having given the men, He then endowed them with the necessary gifts they were to use in His service. There is, however, no uniformity about these gifts. Rather, they represent a unity in diversity: *"Having gifts that differ according to the grace given to us, let us use them"* (Romans 12:6). *"Now there are varieties of gifts, but the same Spirit; and there are varieties of service, but the same Lord; and there are varieties of working, but it is the same God who inspires them all in every one"* (1 Corinthians 12:4–6). *"As each has received a gift, employ it for one another, as good stewards of God's varied grace"* (1 Peter 4:10).

A study of the book of Acts reveals the nature of these manifold gifts bestowed upon believers by the Lord. The greatest gift was that of the Holy Spirit, who, on the day of Pentecost, came as the fulfillment of the promise of Jesus: "*I shall send to you...the Spirit*" (John 15:26). In fact, there is a vital connection between the two declarations "*I will build my church*" (Matthew 16:18) and "*I shall send...the Spirit*," for it was the coming of the Spirit that brought about the establishment and rapid enlargement of the church throughout the first century. In the book of Acts there were also the gifts of power, of boldness, of faith, of wisdom, of tongues, of the ability to preach and teach, and of the ability to suffer. All of the gracious gifts of the Spirit, however, for the perfecting of believers and for carrying out the administrative work of His church and for the building up of His body, are at the disposal of all believers. As Arthur Way translated Ephesians 4:7: "Not indiscriminately, however, on each of us was bestowed the bounty of God's grace, but according to the measure of its bestowal by the Master."

The sum total of such teaching about gifts is that every member of the body of Christ at regeneration receives from the Spirit a gift to use in all future service for the Master. Thus, there is no born-again child of God who does not have a regeneration gift of some kind. The tragedy is that so many who are saved by grace fail to recognize this fact and, consequently, go through their Christian life without using their personal gift for the edification and enrichment of other believers and for the evangelization of the lost.

Is this not the tenor of our Lord's teaching in the parable of the talents (see Matthew 25:14–30) and the parable of the pounds (see Luke 19:12–27)? The man with only one talent hid it in the earth, while the man with only one pound wrapped it up in a napkin. All the others, more gifted, used all that they had received wisely and well, and were thus rewarded. But the man with the one talent, or pound, failing to put it to good use, lost it. These parables depict the action of those who shut up their gifts from the active service of Christ and so retard the progress of the gospel in a world of need. Where are you, personally, in this matter? Have you discovered your regeneration gift, or gifts; and are you employing them to the full for the glory of Him who bestowed them? Or can it be, God forbid, that, since your salvation, which was a gift of grace, your particular gift has been buried in the napkin of neglect? If so, then you will suffer loss when Jesus comes to reward His servants for the use of all He made possible for them. Failure to employ your gift will not mean the loss of eternal life but of the crown of life promised to all who are faithful in life and stewardship. (See James 1:12; Revelation 2:10.)

We may fittingly conclude our consideration of the Pillar of Glorification, of how Jesus was *"taken up in glory,"* by quoting Bishop Horne's comments on Psalm 68:18—*"Thou hast ascended on high"* (KJV)—the prophetic Scripture that Paul quoted in Ephesians 4:8 to describe our Lord's ascension gifts:

> Thou, O Christ, who didst descend from the right hand of the Majesty of the heavens to the lower parts of the earth, art again ascended from the lower parts of the earth to the right hand of the Majesty in the heavens; *"thou hast led captivity captive"*; thou hast conquered the conqueror, bound the strong one, redeemed human nature from the grave, and triumphantly carried it, with thee, to the throne of God; *"thou hast received gifts for men; yea, for the rebellious also"*; and being thus ascended into thy glory, thou hast received of the Father the promise of the Spirit, with all his gifts and graces, to bestow upon the sons of men; even upon such as heretofore have not only broken thy laws, but appeared in arms against thee; yet of such as these, converted by the power of thy gospel, wilt thou form and establish a church; *"that the LORD God may dwell among them"*; that so, of thy faithful people, gathered from all parts of the world, may be built up a living temple, *"an habitation of God through the Spirit."*[81]

---

81. Horne, *Commentary on the Book of Psalms*, 270–271.

CONCLUSION

THE FUNDAMENTAL SPIRITUAL VALUE OF THE MYSTERY WE CONFESS

We began our consideration of the timeless confession-chant that Paul quoted in his first epistle to Timothy by exploring that great mystery of the faith, the virgin birth of our Lord, to which the apostle referred as he introduced the vital truths that follow. As we conclude our sacred meditation, we return again to that mystery, because the more it is studied, the more clearly it will be seen that the entire doctrine of the incarnation, that "[God] *was manifested in the flesh*," and all that follows from this, depends on this mystery in a most vital and central way.

There are those who would have us believe that the virgin birth has no important doctrinal value connected with it, and that belief in it is not to be regarded as essential to the acceptance of the Christian faith. As Professor Orr so eloquently put it:

> It is a fair question to raise, whether or not the evidence justifies belief in the virgin birth. But it seems to me self-evident that, if the virgin birth is believed to be true, it must be held to be an essential element in the Incarnation, as it actually happened. It was the way in which God chose to bring about the Incarnation, and it cannot but be vitally connected with the fact of which it was the instrumental cause.[82]

---

82. James Orr, *The Virgin Birth of Christ* (New York: Scribner's, 1907), 234.

That we can and must believe the virgin birth to be true, and that it is indeed an essential element of the incarnation and vitally connected with it, will now be our purpose to prove.

THE VIRGIN BIRTH IS THE FOUNDATION OF THE GOSPEL

The superstructure of the life and character of our Lord Jesus Christ has as its immovable and only foundation His virgin birth. Other foundation can no man lay and still retain the Savior that the Bible portrays.

If Christ was born of human parents, or, in other words, if there was nothing miraculous about His birth, such as being conceived by the Holy Spirit suggests, or if the New Testament narratives are not genuine but full of mistakes, or of deliberate, intentional fabrication, or of mythical folklore, then we are shut up to some solemn and tragic conclusions:

If Jesus was not conceived by the Holy Spirit and born of a virgin, then Mary's character is blasted; and her child would be stamped as the offspring of lust and shame, for He was born out of wedlock.

If Jesus was not conceived by the Holy Spirit and born of a virgin, then He is not the Holy One whom we believe Him to be, for never in the history of mankind has natural generation produced a sinless being.

Rejection of Christ's holy birth means the rejection of His holy, spotless life. As Professor A. B. Bruce said, "With belief in the virgin birth is apt to go belief in the virgin life....A sinless man is as much a miracle in the moral world as a virgin birth is a miracle in the physical world."[83] In his article on the virgin birth in *The Fundamentals*, Professor Orr said:

Doctrinally, it must be repeated that the belief in the virgin birth of Christ is of the highest value for the right apprehension of Christ's unique and sinless personality. Here is One, as Paul brings out in Romans 5:12, who, free from sin Himself and not involved in the Adamic liabilities of the race, reverses the curse of sin and death brought in by the first Adam, and establishes the reign of righteousness and life. Had Christ been naturally born, not one of these things could be affirmed of Him. As one of Adam's race, not an entrant from a higher sphere, He would have shared in Adam's corruption and doom—would Himself have required to be

83. Alexander Balmain Bruce, *Apologetics* (Edinburgh: T. & T. Clark, 1892), 410.